MW01626307

The American Horse

The American Horse

at Frederik Meijer Gardens & Sculpture Park

Larry ten Harmsel

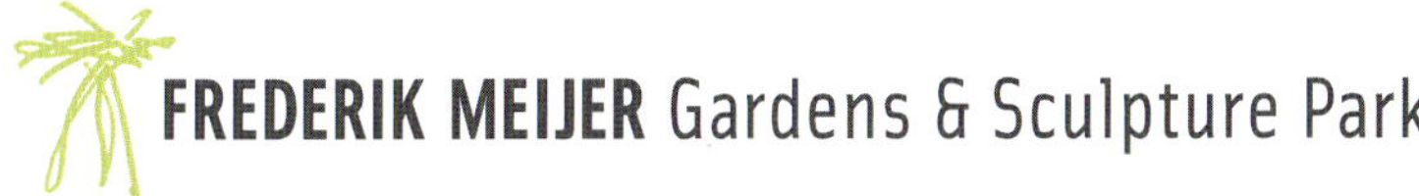

Published 2010 by
Frederik Meijer Gardens & Sculpture Park
1000 E. Beltline Ave. NE, Grand Rapids, Michigan 49525

Manufactured in the United States of America

15 14 13 12 11 10 5 4 3 2 1

ISBN 978-0-9827824-0-8

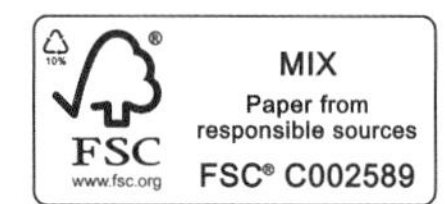

Contents

Acknowledgments

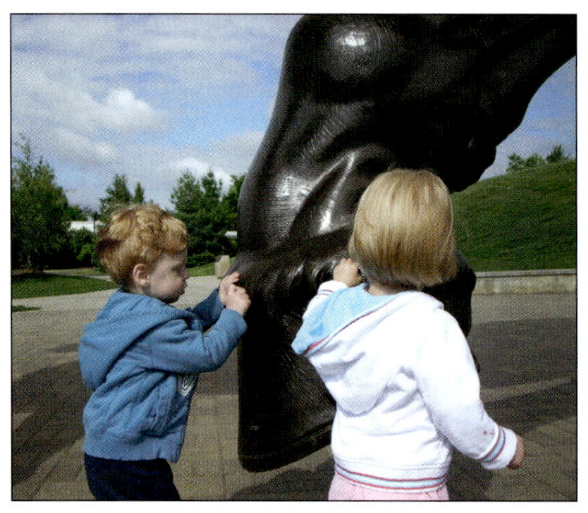

There are many people who deserve thanks for sharing their experience, offering their advice, and giving their support. The countless contributions of Fred and Lena Meijer are merely hinted at in the text. At Meijer Gardens, I am especially indebted to David Hooker, Joe Becherer, Roger Bleiler, Bob Kinney, Marlene Vanderhill, and Tammy Freehling. At Eerdmans Publishing Company Reinder Van Til, Linda Bieze, and Klaas Wolterstorff provided sterling services. I am especially grateful to Nina Akamu. Without her, neither *The American Horse* nor this story of its creation could have come into being.

Larry ten Harmsel
April 26, 2010

Introduction

When children first see it they run to it, congregating beneath the overhead torso, hugging the tree-like legs, hammering on the massive hooves, staring up at the expressive face. The adults who accompany these children may approach more slowly, progressively entranced by the massive size, impressed by its muscularity, its passion, or the supreme sense of control implied in its form. For many visitors to Frederik Meijer Gardens & Sculpture Park, *The American Horse* is their first encounter with the exhilarating, challenging experience of sculpture that this institution can provide.

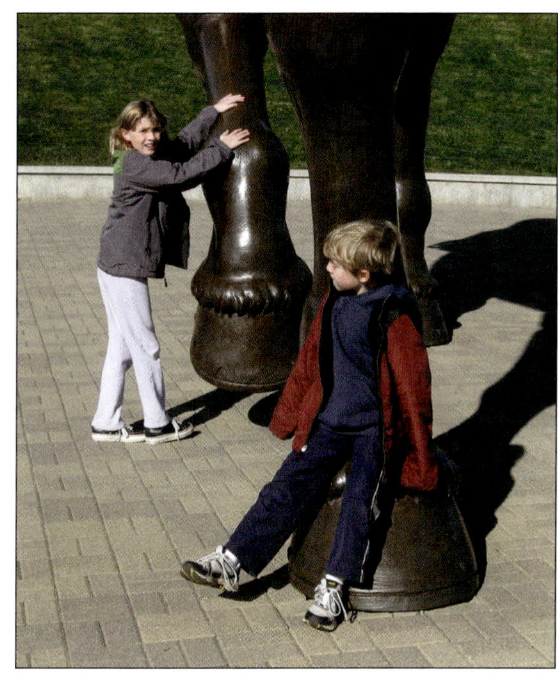

How did this horse come to be? More importantly, how did it come to be in Grand Rapids, Michigan? The story is long and complicated, with as many false starts and dead ends as a labyrinth. This small book attempts to explain the long history behind the creation of *The American Horse,* how it came to be displayed on a broad terrace of Frederik Meijer Gardens & Sculpture Park, and how its presence has played a role in expanding and developing one of the world's premier cultural institutions.

1. The Meijer Connection

Retailer and philanthropist Fred Meijer often sought to support cultural projects that could stir the imagination and celebrate creativity. In 1995, after a long process of planning and fundraising, he had presided over the grand opening of the institution now named for him, Frederik Meijer Gardens & Sculpture Park.

A year later, in 1996, the ambitious undertaking was off to a good start. There were newly planted gardens at the 80-acre site, which would need years to mature. There was a pathway through the woods and along the wetlands, a small pond coated with duckweed, a winding swale that became a little creek after a rainstorm, all of which demonstrated the diversity of landscapes available on the still undeveloped site. There was the five-story Lena Meijer Conservatory, the largest of its kind in Michigan. It was buttressed by support greenhouses, allowing it to display a variety of tropical plants and, each spring, a mesmerizing show of tropical butterflies soaring through the heights of the great glass box.

There was also the kernel of a sculpture collection, showing a longtime interest Fred had developed in this three-dimensional art form. It had long been clear that his wife, Lena, was the gardener in the family. He was more interested in sculpture, and had donated the initial 80 acres (it would eventually grow to 132 acres) for the express purpose of displaying his sculpture collection within Meijer Gardens. For many years, he had housed much of that collection in a warehouse near the Meijer corporate headquarters, where it lay on the floor in a state of

Meijer, Inc., is a major Midwest retailer. The company's grocery and general merchandise stores average 200,000 square feet each (or about the size of four regular grocery stores) and stock about 120,000 items. A family-owned business, with 62,000 employees, Meijer operates some 200 stores; approximately half of them are in Michigan, while the rest are in Illinois, Indiana, Kentucky, and Ohio. Stores comprise more than forty departments, including apparel, electronics, hardware, and toys. Most also sell gasoline and offer pharmacy services. Founder Hendrik Meijer (1883-1964) opened his first store in 1934; his son Fred (b. 1919) worked with him from the beginning.

benign neglect. He had long looked for ways to display it appropriately, but felt stymied.

Even before Meijer Gardens opened, Meijer had created a Sculpture Advisory Committee whose purpose was to offer advice and counsel about artistic direction. Chaired by Lynn Vinkemulder, a friend and collector, the committee included people with both academic and practical sculptural experience. An early member of that committee, Henry Matthews, remembers going with Meijer to visit what amounted to an expanded pole barn. Matthews is currently curator of art for Grand Valley State University, but in 1996 he was the Director of the Muskegon Museum of Art.

"The first time I went to that warehouse with Fred, he showed me this pile of Marshall Fredericks stuff. I knew Fredericks's work and knew of his importance in Michigan art. But the real point is, I was meeting the most amazing individual — Fred — whose interests had come to include sculpture, for some reason."

Fred and Lena had begun collecting some years earlier, when they met the artist Marshall Fredericks in Fred's home town of Greenville. For years thereafter, they had acquired additional pieces done by Fredericks, a significant figure in American figurative art. (His best-known work is probably the gigantic *Spirit of Detroit* that stands in front of the City-County building in downtown Detroit.) Many of Fredericks's creations were on display as Meijer Gardens celebrated its first year of existence. The Meijers had also collected a number of pieces by other sculptors that were purely decorative, thinking perhaps they would enhance a garden setting.

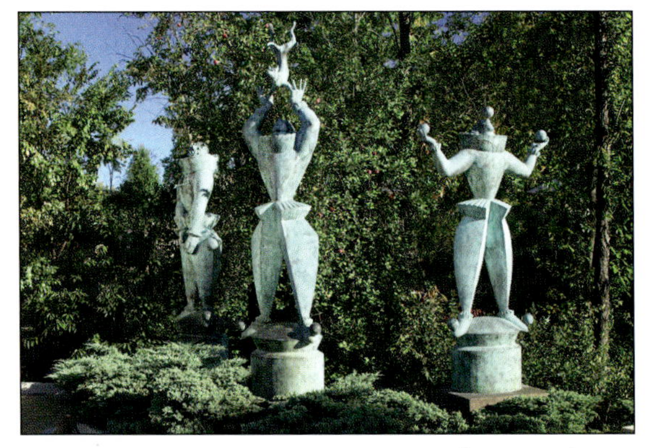

Marshall Fredericks. *Three Clowns,* 1938 (Cast 1991)

Photo by William J. Hebert

One other element of this early collection was its focus on animal sculpture. A goat, a frog, a toad, a wolf, a cow, a pig, a crow, a fox, a bear: images that called to mind his bucolic childhood and youth. These and dozens of other examples (all of them now gracing Michigan's Farm Garden and the Lena Meijer Children's Garden) were included in the initial array of holdings.

By 1996, though, Meijer also saw the need for the institution to develop in some new directions. There was a feeling that it didn't have enough variety in its offerings, that it would take years for the plantings to reach maturity, and that the parking lots would never stay full the way things stood. Meijer had learned a great deal about filling parking lots in his retail business, and wanted to see what he could do on that front for this new public cultural organization. It was time to grow.

In the late summer of 1996, Fred's son Hank showed him an article from the *New York Times*. Datelined Beacon, New York, it outlined a tantalizing story:

> *This small Hudson River city, a warren of alternately forlorn and quaintly restored Victorian precincts, seems a universe apart from Milan — chic, sophisticated, bustling Milan.*
>
> *But a dream that started in that northern Italian city is being realized in this town about 60 miles north of New York City.*
>
> *It is a true labyrinthine tale that started 500 years ago with Leonardo da Vinci and a horse. Not just any horse, but a 24-foot-tall bronze charger that Leonardo conceived but never completed.*
>
> *Today, a full-scale model of the horse stands frozen mid-stride, veins popping, muscles bulging, in a vast foundry here.*

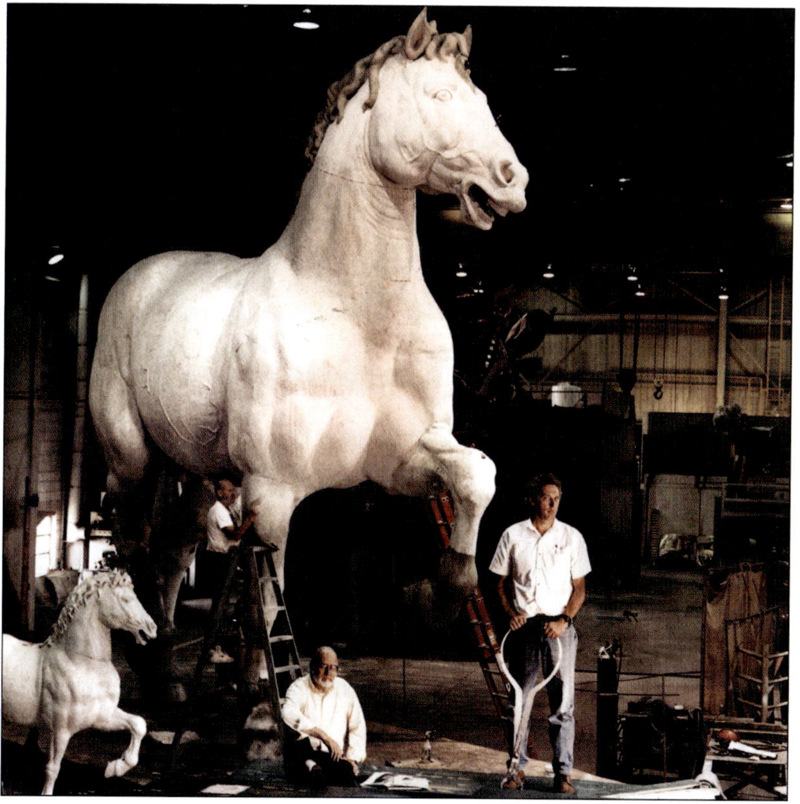

The Dent horse, with alterations being attempted

Immediately, Meijer was drawn to the project's grand proportions — this sort of attraction could fill the parking lots. He was also drawn to the iconic name of Leonardo, perhaps the most illustrious of the many all-round geniuses active during the Renaissance. In addition, he had always appreciated animal imagery. Farm animals, and especially horses, played a prominent part in Fred's childhood in Greenville, where he grew up on a farm in the days just before the internal combustion engine replaced old-fashioned horsepower.

Soon the Meijer corporate plane was on its way to visit the storied Tallix Foundry in Beacon. But before describing what stood in the foundry, it is necessary to provide some ancient history, as background to the modern drama about to unfold.

2. Leonardo's Role

A history of the horse involves ambition, desire, dynastic power, money, frustration, destruction, and creativity on two continents. To tell the tale with anything approaching the truth means going back more than five hundred years, and even then there are complications. For one thing, the original horse, as Leonardo imagined and designed it, doesn't exist. A full-scale model was destroyed by French soldiers in 1499. But that's getting ahead of the story. Let's begin at the beginning.

Francesco Sforza (1401-1466) oversaw his family's tumultuous entry into the world of power politics in the Italian peninsula near the beginning of the Renaissance — that flowering of culture from which both modern democracy and modern capitalism arose. Francesco was a condottiere — a kind of mercenary warlord who hired his army out to the highest bidder in a time when the Italian city-states were perennially at war with each other.

He was a hard negotiator and fierce commander, so famous that he became one of the featured characters in Machiavelli's classic political handbook, *The Prince*. On one occasion, for example, he began a battle by fighting against Pope Nicholas V's Roman army and, after some negotiations that made him a much richer man, ended the battle on the Pope's victorious side.

In 1450, as Milan suffered from famine and rioting in the streets, the Milanese Senate gave Francesco the title Duke of Milan. The Church in Rome, by this time his enemy again, did not approve. But he managed to calm the city's tensions and bring a

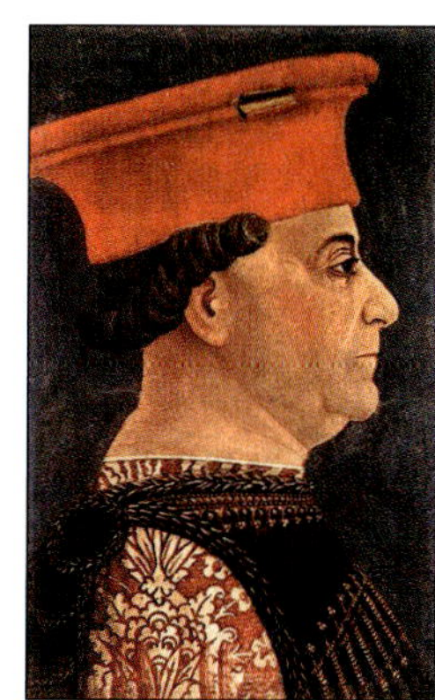

Francesco Sforza , by Bonifacio Bembo

Pinacoteca di Brera / Wikimedia

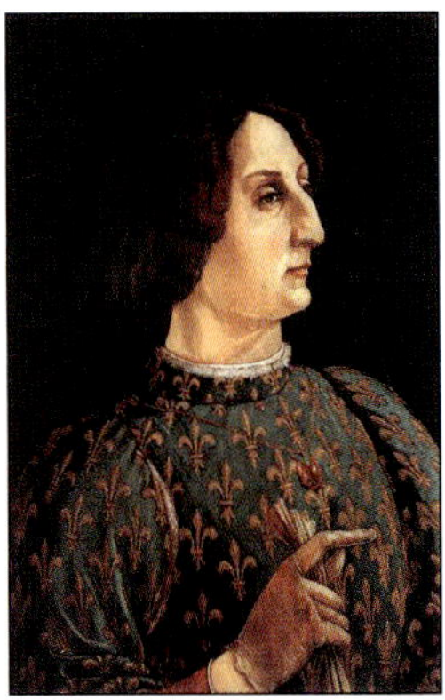

Galeazzo Maria Sforza, by Piero Pollaiuolo
Galleria d'Uffizi / Wikimedia

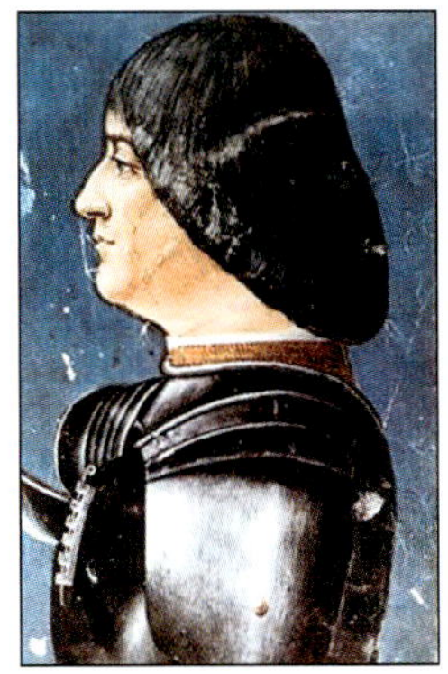

Ludovico Sforza, by Giovanni di Predis
Cleveland Museum of Art / Wikimedia

period of peace and prosperity, for which he was widely admired. He formed alliances throughout the Italian peninsula and worked to balance the power of potential enemies and preserve Milan's stability. During his rule, his city-state began to play a significant role in European politics.

His moderate policies of government, his system of taxation, and his support for humanitarian causes and the arts made him an important figure in the emerging Italian Renaissance. During this time Cosimo de Medici was the ruler of Florence, and the two men got along famously. Francesco's stability and his powerful connections allowed him to establish a dynasty in the province of Lombardy. And that is how the dysfunctional Sforza family came to rule in Milan, where it flourished and fought for several generations.

After Francesco's death in 1466, his eldest son Galeazzo Maria (1444-1476) became Duke. His violent, careless reign lasted for ten years. Noted for such cruelties as nailing a living man into a coffin, and killing a poacher by forcing him to eat a dead rabbit, skin and all, Galeazzo Maria was assassinated by political opponents on the day after Christmas, 1476, while kneeling in church.

Soon the reins of power passed to Francesco's second son, Ludovico Sforza (1452-1508), known as *Il Moro* ("the Moor"). He was a masterful manipulator who engineered alliances and marriages with many of Europe's most important families, and kept spies (he called them "diplomats") in the major courts of Europe.

Ludovico, like his father Francesco, was a great supporter of the arts. In that capacity he attracted a number of artists to the court of Milan. Among them was the greatest genius of the era, Leonardo da Vinci. In 1482 Leonardo came to Milan to work for Ludovico. His letter of application has become a classic, widely quoted in histories of the time. Describing himself, Leonardo demonstrates every kind of talent except modesty.

To Ludovico Il Moro:

Most illustrious Lord, I shall endeavor, without prejudice to any one else, to explain myself to your Excellency, showing your Lordship my secrets, and then offering them to your best pleasure and approbation to work with effect at opportune moments as well as all those things which, in part, shall be briefly noted below.

He goes on at great length, boasting of his skill in warfare on land or at sea, listing weapons systems of his own invention: covered chariots, big guns, catapults, all sorts of military inventions.

— *In time of peace I believe I can give perfect satisfaction and to the equal of any other in architecture and the composition of buildings public and private; and in guiding water from one place to another.*

— *Item: I can carry out sculpture in marble, bronze or clay, and also in painting whatever may be done, and as well as any other, be he whom he may.*

It may have been boasting, but it was accurate. As an engineer of war machines, tunnels, irrigation methods, architectural defenses, and armaments, Leonardo had no peer. Once in Milan, his first assignment was to design a monument to the memory of Francesco Sforza.

Initially it was planned as a life-sized equestrian statue, showing a victorious warrior on a horse. One preliminary sketch showed vanquished foes being trampled on by the horse. But the idea kept changing, and Leonardo, already known as someone who seldom finished his projects, always found something else to do for the Duke.

In the midst of a host of other projects — wars, treaties, a new hospital for

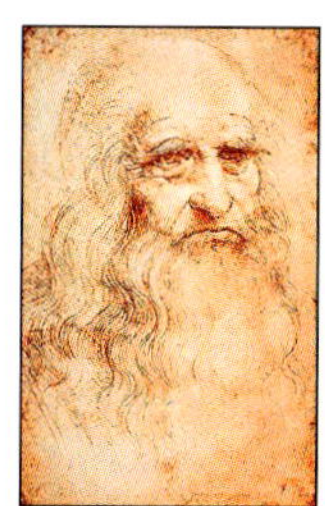

Anyone who's aware of Dan Brown's best-selling novel *The Da Vinci Code* might well think that the artist was known in his own day as "Da Vinci." In fact, this giant of the Renaissance (like his illustrious peers Michelangelo and Raphael) was generally known by his first name, Leonardo. His birth name was Leonardo di Ser Piero (Leonardo son of Sir Piero). Since he had been born in the small Tuscan town of Vinci, he was also referred to as "Leonardo from Vinci" (Leonardo da Vinci), but during his lifetime he would never have been called "Da Vinci" without his first name.

the city's poor — Ludovico kept increasing the size of the memorial, to the point where the horse alone would be some 24 feet high. By that time, his ego had also done away with the idea of honoring his father by placing him on horseback. Now, with his brother out of the way and himself firmly planted in power, it was simply going to be the Sforza monument, the largest bronze horse anywhere in the world. It would require more than 60 tons of metal for casting, and Leonardo set about making studies and sketches. Michelangelo, working in Florence and Rome, heard about these grandiose notions and told anyone who would listen that it was impossible. Nothing so large had ever been cast in one piece, and he didn't believe it could be done.

In response, Leonardo made elaborate casting plans. He would place the mold upside down and below ground level in the castle's spacious courtyard. He would arrange for special vents to minimize deformity as the bronze cooled. He would allow several months for the molten metal to congeal. He would see to every detail, so that nothing went wrong.

In 1493, eleven years after arriving in Milan, Leonardo completed a full-sized clay model of the horse. He was now painfully close to seeing this enormous project at an end. All that was needed was for the Duke to stockpile 60 tons of bronze.

Leonardo engaged himself in imagining where the colossus might be placed, either on the battlements of the castle or on a pedestal nearby. He imagined it, taller than a two-story building, visible from a great distance, gleaming in the sun. But fate had other plans for him and his horse.

Between 1495 and 1498, as the Duke was amassing the last of the needed bronze, Leonardo painted "The Last Supper," one of the best-known images in the world, on the wall of the refectory at Santa Maria delle Grazie.

As for the tons of bronze, his employer came up with yet another idea. Sensing a threat from France, Ludovico planned a major military offensive, which would expand his territory and make him virtually impervious to all enemies. He needed the bronze to make cannon. Leonardo's sculpture would have to wait.

Although there wasn't much he could say about it publicly, Leonardo's dream had shrunk, in the space of just a few months, to nothing more than a clay model. As it turned out, Ludovico's war efforts failed. In 1499, after a long siege, the French army entered the city, captured the Duke, and put an end to both his reign and Leonardo's dream. During the occupation, French archers used Leonardo's clay model for target practice, reducing it to a pile of burnt-orange shards. Now nothing was left.

Leonardo closed down his Milanese operations and left for Venice. He then returned to Florence for a few years, and in 1516 he accepted an offer to move to France. He joined the court of Francis I, the newly crowned King, who was bent on importing the Renaissance to France. Leonardo took with him a few belongings, including the *Mona Lisa.* It was in France that he died in 1519, the horse nothing more than a distant memory. And that was apparently the end of the story.

The notebooks in which he had drawn up his plans seemed for centuries to have disappeared, although rumors surfaced from time to time about sketches found in one or another royal collection, in England, France, or Spain.

3. A Sort of Resurrection

There the story rested for more than four hundred years. In early 1967, two leather-bound volumes of Leonardo's notebooks — 700 pages in all — were discovered by accident in the National Library of Madrid. A researcher, Professor Jules Piccus of the University of Massachusetts, had been looking for medieval ballads and had stumbled on this woefully miscatalogued treasure. Scholars had a field day.

Among other things, they came across twenty pages of notes and sketches detailing how Leonardo hoped to cast his equine monument. A decade later, in 1977, *National Geographic* published a lengthy article about Leonardo's accomplishments. One part of the story, a small feature called "The Horse That Never Was," told the sad saga of Leonardo's uncompleted horse.

That story captured the imagination of a retired United Airlines pilot, Charles Dent (1917-1994), an art collector and adventurer from the Lehigh Valley in Pennsylvania, who thought there should be some way to complete this 500-year-old project. He called a few friends to his farmhouse in Fogelsburg, Pennsylvania, and said, in effect, "Let's give Leonardo his horse."

Dent organized a nonprofit corporation, Leonardo Da Vinci's Horse, Inc. (LDVHI). His exuberant idea was to create an equine colossus in the spirit of Leonardo's and to give it to

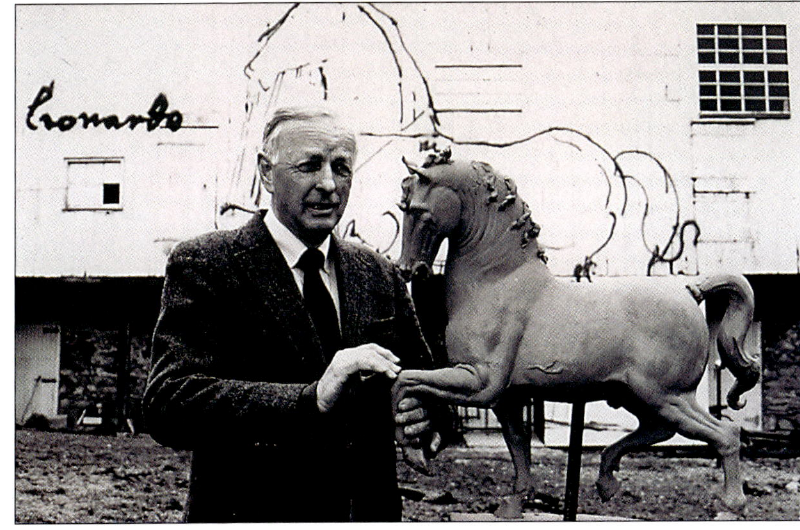

Charles Dent with a model of his horse

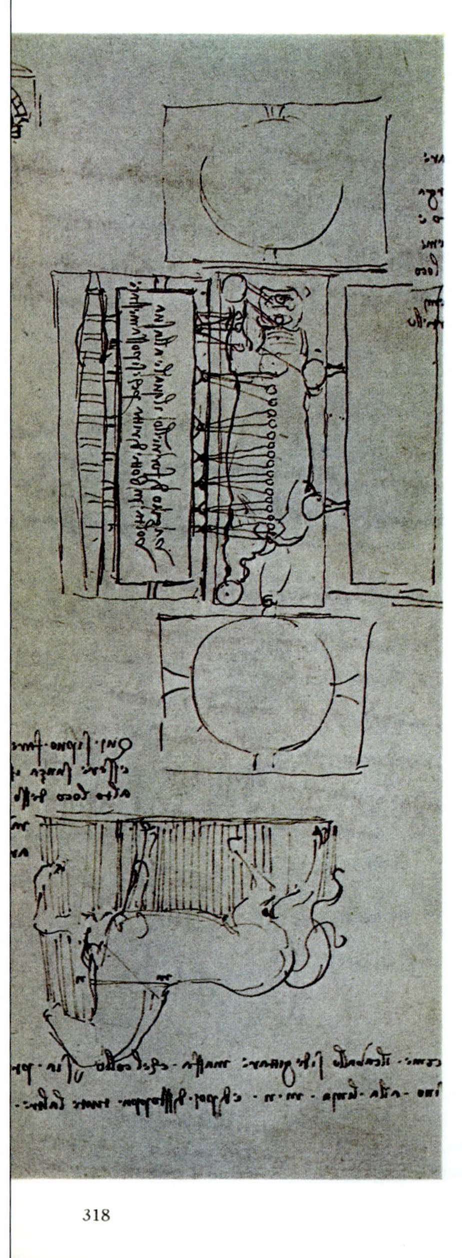

THE HORSE THAT NEVER WAS

LEONARDO'S Milan patron, Lodovico Sforza, demanded the world's largest statue, a 23-foot-high bronze horse with rider, to be placed in a courtyard of his castle in Milan (**right**). With meticulous attention to detail, Leonardo sketched animals in the Sforza stables, then constructed a huge clay model, and finally devised a radically new process to cast the horse in a single operation. Iron framing (**below**) held the plaster mold for the head.

The molds were to be buried upside down, between circular ovens (**left**). Molten bronze—an incredible 79 tons—would pour through tubes into the molds (**lower left**).

Before casting could proceed, however, war intervened. Lodovico took the bronze to make cannon; in 1499 he lost to French armies, who occupied the castle and used the clay horse for archery practice. Just 200 years later French designers fashioned an equestrian statue of Louis XIV. Smaller but similar to Leonardo's design, it employed his casting technique. The method is still used.

BOTH DRAWINGS BIBLIOTECA NACIONAL, MADRID; TED SPIEGEL, BLACK STAR (RIGHT)

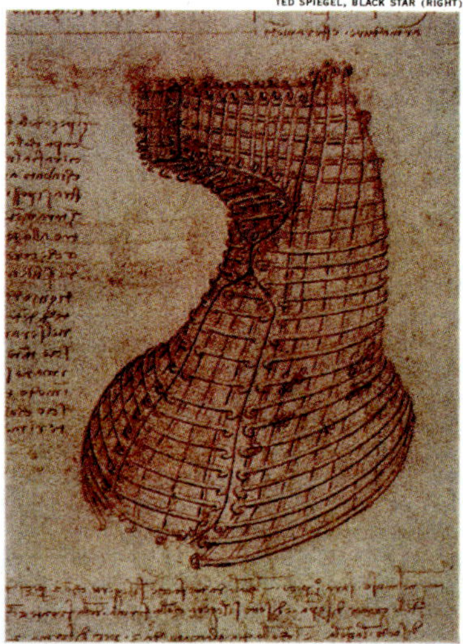

318 *National Geographic, September 1977*

"Leonardo da Vinci: A Man for All Ages – The Horse That Never Was," *National Geographic*, September 1977. Used by Permission.

the people of Milan as a token of America's appreciation for the Italian Renaissance and for the contributions Italians had made to America over the centuries.

Dent saw this gift as a parallel, in some ways, to the Statue of Liberty, which had been given to America by the French. Dent met with scholars and politicians in America and Italy, and by 1980 he had begun work on an eight-foot version of the horse that he hoped to cast. However, Dent was not an artist, and his early models of the horse failed to pass muster with scholars who looked at them. When Dent realized that he did not have the skill to sculpt the work himself, he asked others to help.

Rod Skidmore, a watercolorist who specialized in racehorses, was brought into the process. Skidmore realized quickly that his experience did not give him the ability to add much to the work of sculpting, though he remained a valuable member of the LDVHI foundation. Students at nearby schools occasionally pitched in, and "Leonardo's Horse" soon became a committee project, taking on different shapes and forms, and finally resulting in an eight-foot plaster model that would eventually be enlarged in an attempt to create the monumental horse. Meanwhile, LDVHI kept raising funds.

By 1991, the group had raised enough money to make molds and cast a few eight-foot plaster models to use for further publicity. One of these models was covered in gold paint and placed on a pedestal at Dent's farm.

Dent himself, however, suffered from a bad heart, and his condition was complicated by ALS, Lou Gehrig's Disease. He died on Christmas day, 1994, fearful that his desire to give a monument to the Italian people might die with him. The board members who were at his bedside promised to do everything in their power to bring his dream to completion. Dent's brother-in-law, Charles Enloe, became chairman of the committee, and his emotional investment in the project was infectious. There was

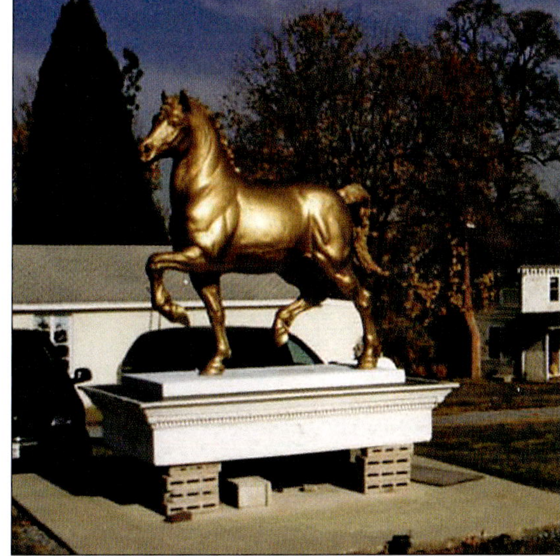

The Dent horse, gilded Photo by Larry ten Harmsel

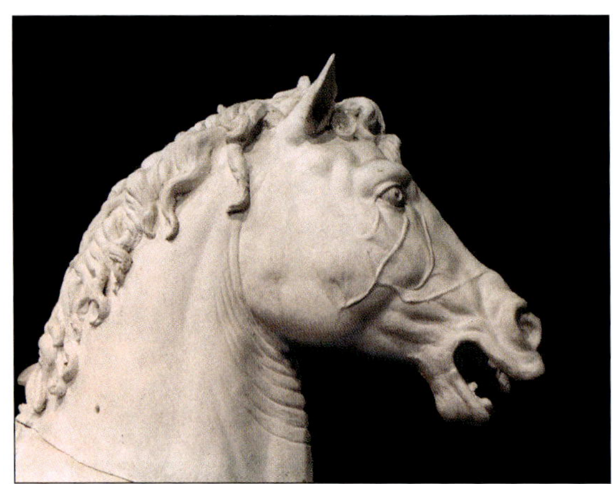

Dent horse – head and mane Photo by Nina Akamu

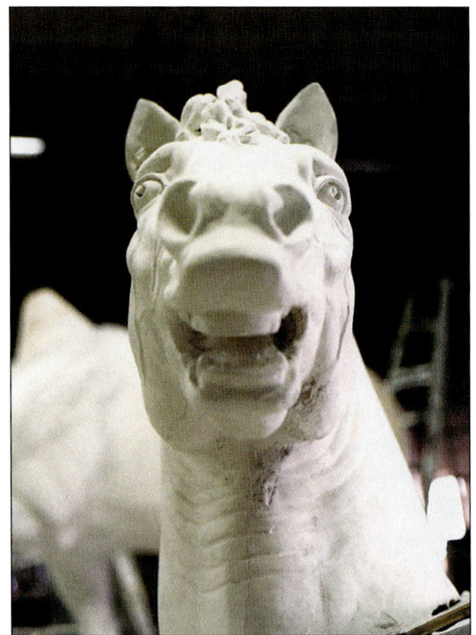

Front view Photo by Nina Akamu

now enough money to send the eight-foot horse to the Tallix Foundry, one of the country's premier art foundries, in Beacon, New York. The LDVHI foundation could not yet afford to cast it in bronze, but they were able to complete the next step, a full-size plaster model. After that was completed, the fundraising would have to begin again, using the enlargement as an inducement to potential backers.

Greg Glasson, a transplanted South African sculptor who was President of Tallix at the time, set the foundry to work enlarging the eight-foot horse. But problems arose very quickly. When a piece of sculpture is enlarged to three times its former size, flaws and distortions, which might not be obvious at the smaller size, become painfully clear. Within a month, a twenty-four-foot horse stood in the foundry's large warehouse, dwarfing everything around it, and Glasson was faced with a new crisis: the horse was a monstrosity.

Two of its four legs — the ones raised in the air — were the wrong length. The left front was too short to reach the ground, while the right rear was too long. The four hooves were four different sizes; the ears were tiny, more like those of a squirrel than a horse; the eyeballs were wildly askew, the skull lopsided, and there were masses of muscle that bore no relationship to what is found in the anatomy of living horses.

To make matters worse, Dent and his friends had based their work on American quarter horses, while Leonardo had patterned his drawings on the regal Iberian horses found in the stables of the Duke of Milan. Lippizaner stallions, trained in Vienna, are perhaps the best-known Iberians in the modern era. They have a physiology different from quarter horses in many significant ways, which is part of the reason they are able to perform their striking maneuvers.

"It was a tricky situation," said Glasson, "because when a project comes to the foundry, it's not the foundry's position to tell the artist his work is not well sculpted — our job is simply to cast it. And the problem was made worse because this particular project was to have an international profile and would be important to a large public. It was going to Italy as a gift from America.

"A lot of artists working at the foundry, including many credible figurative sculptors, members of the National Sculpture Society, would occasionally walk past the horse as it was being enlarged. They expressed a concern that it would be an embarrassment to America."

The Tallix board of directors, primarily focused on the fiscal health of the business, tried to ease Glasson's concerns by agreeing to let him hire someone to fix the problems, so long as it was paid for by LDVHI. Glasson approached a longtime acquaintance, the sculptor Nina Akamu. Born in Oklahoma and trained in classical techniques at the Maryland Institute College of Art, Akamu was uniquely suited to this particular project. She had studied in Italy for twelve years, concentrating on the work of many of Leonardo's contemporaries. In addition, the foundry had worked with her, and the members respected her dedication and talent. (She did not know it at the time, but she was about to be chosen to execute the national memorial for interned Japanese Americans in Washington, D.C.) She agreed to come in for a look at the massive horse.

"I went to see it," Akamu said,

with Annina Nosei, a gallery owner, and Athos Ongaro, an Italian sculptor. We entered the foundry, and when we turned a corner and saw the sculpture, Annina said, "O Dio — che brutto!" ("Lord, that's ugly!"). She was very offended, in dramatic Italian fashion, by what she saw. We examined it in some detail, and saw that it was very ama-

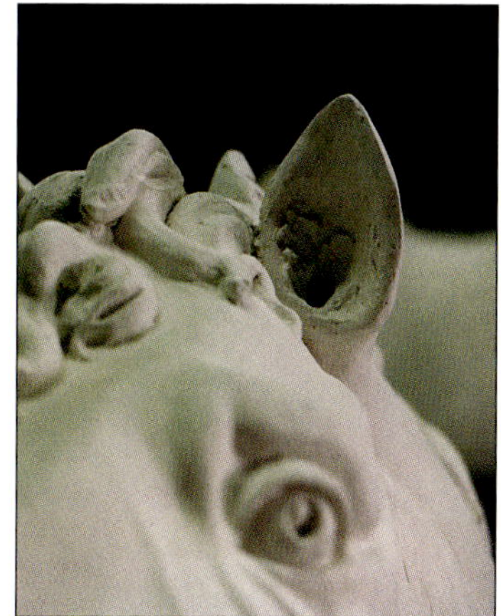

Small ear Photo by Nina Akamu

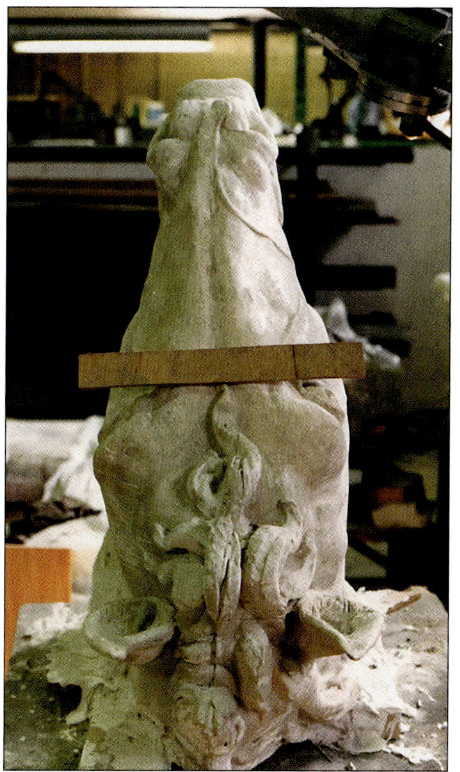

Asymmetrical eyes Photo by Nina Akamu

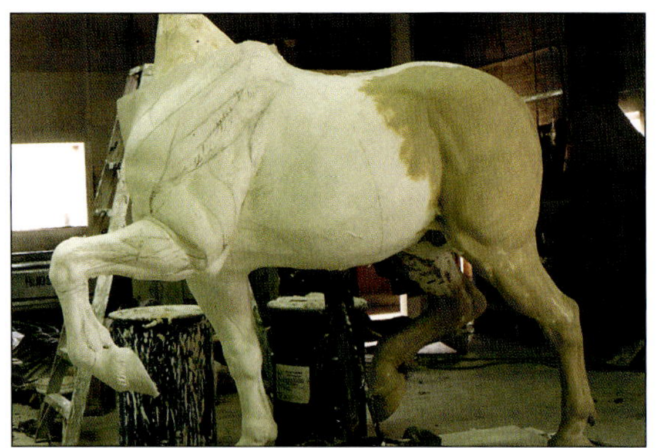

Dent horse – marking musculature Photo by Nina Akamu

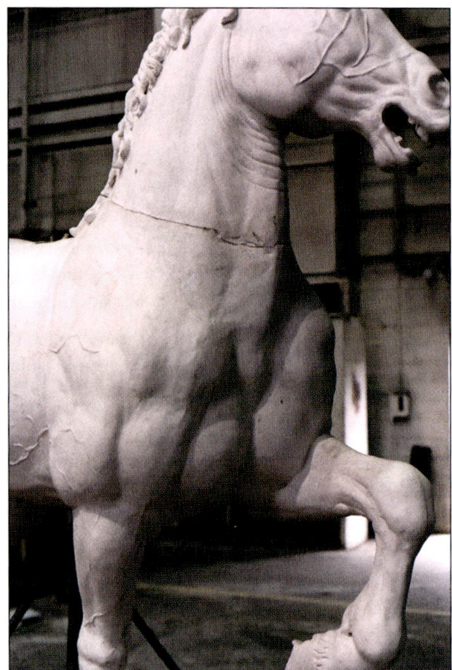

Veins and sinews Photo by Nina Akamu

teurish and had a lot of anatomical problems. It was badly imagined in almost every conceivable way.

Even the thought of trying to fix small areas of it struck me as impossible. The problems were not small or superficial. I didn't give it a second thought. I told Greg I wasn't interested in working on this project. I thought that was the end of it.

But that was not the end of it. Within a few months, the *New York Times* featured an article talking about Charles Dent's dream, accompanied by a picture of the plaster model. After reporting parenthetically that the foundry was completing a statue of Franklin D. Roosevelt to be placed in Washington, D.C., the *Times* went on to say that "workers at Tallix, with the help of an enlarging device known as a pantograph, have completed a twenty-four-foot-tall plaster and clay model of the horse. With a few refinements, the enormous equine — about eight feet wide and twenty-four feet long — will be ready to be cast in bronze soon."

There was no hint of how significant those "few refinements" were to be, no sense that this peculiar stallion was never to be cast in bronze.

4. Finding a Sculptor

Nina Akamu saw the picture of Dent's horse in the August 18, 1996, edition of the *New York Times.* "I couldn't believe it was still alive, and that Tallix planned to cast it," she said.

"Greg called me in again, and his sheer persistence convinced me to work on the big sculpture for three months, to try to fix it. LDVHI did not have enough money to make the enlargement in Plastilene clay. Instead, they made it of Structolite, a construction material combining concrete and plaster. The surface of the enlargement was so rough it would take your skin off if you rubbed up against it."

With serious misgivings, Akamu agreed to take on the task, thinking it would only last three months.

"My first job," she recalled, "was to create a hoof they could use to demonstrate the size of the horse. That was to be cast in resin and used as a showpiece, to market the story of Leonardo's horse, and try to raise more money.

"At that point we were just worried about the most basic elements of horse anatomy, and not dealing at all with ideas related to Leonardo. That horse had no basis in Leonardo's work.

"I was just coming in as an anonymous ghost sculptor, looking at anatomy and nothing else. I was to be paid by the hour. I didn't really think this project was going to go anywhere, and I

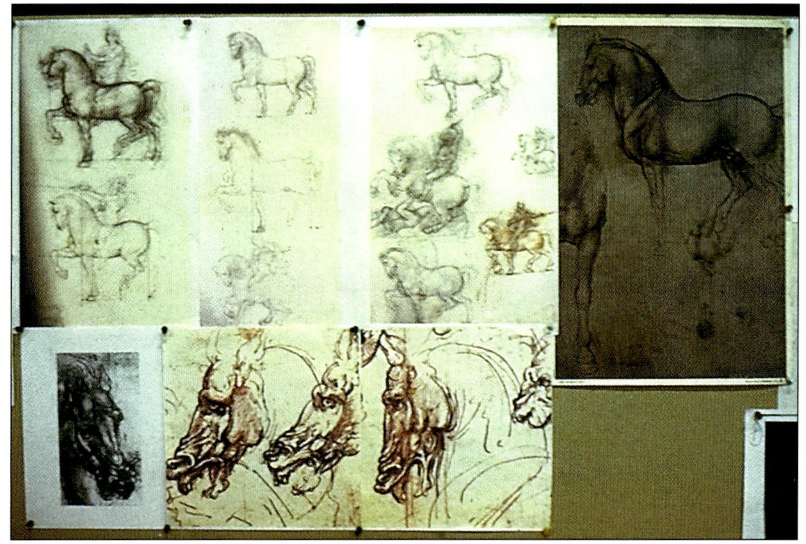

Nina Akamu's bulletin board Photo by Larry ten Harmsel

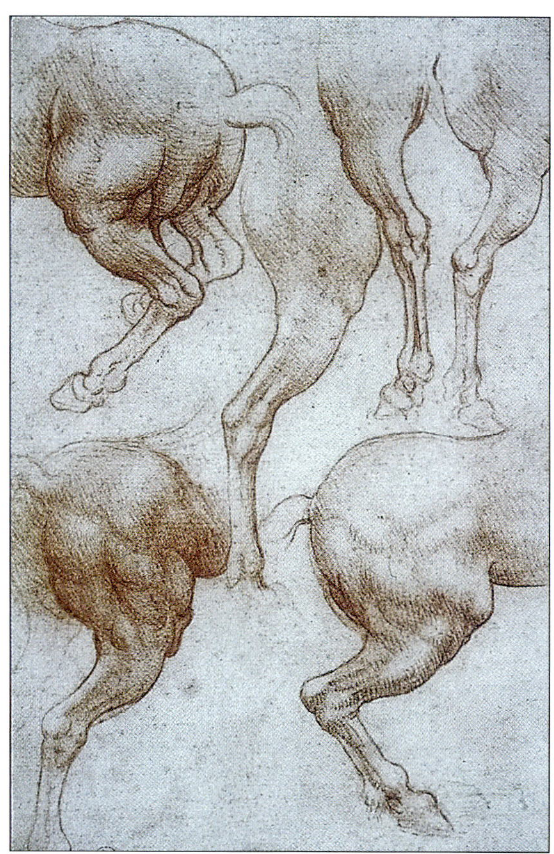

Detail of Leonardo drawings

Royal Collection at Windsor Castle / Wikimedia

took great consolation in the fact that I was anonymous, because that horse was so embarrassing. That's sort of what I thought about the project when I first started it. Then it took on a life of its own. It was not about sculpting a horse, or doing a 'Leonardo'; it was about a great challenge, lots of them that had nothing to do with the horse. It was more about a *process.* The challenge of doing the impossible, whatever that challenge might be for the day."

The massive twenty-four-foot charger on the foundry floor was about to suffer the same fate that had befallen Leonardo's clay model 500 years earlier. Instead of being used for target practice by French soldiers, this one would be destroyed by critics, not the least of whom was Nina Akamu herself. But she would go on to create a new version, based not only on Leonardo's drawings but also on her extensive studies of other Renaissance equine and equestrian statues.

Meanwhile, Fred Meijer saw the story about Leonardo's horse in the *New York Times.* Less than a year earlier, he had presided over the opening of Frederik Meijer Gardens & Sculpture Park in Grand Rapids, and he found the *Times* article fascinating. He thought it would be a wonderful thing for Americans to give such a gift to the people of Italy, and he also imagined that having a copy of the sculpture in Grand Rapids would bring people to Meijer Gardens.

Fred arranged to take a half dozen members of Meijer Gardens' Sculpture Advisory Committee with him to the Tallix Foundry to look at the horse and to discuss the possibility of supporting it financially. The committee was unanimous in pronouncing it unfit. They saw the same things that had worried people at the foundry and had spurred the hiring of Akamu in the first place. Everyone agreed the sculpture was a disaster.

But the romance behind it — the idea of mounting a project that had languished for five centuries — still had great appeal.

Fred Meijer loved the narrative — if not the sculpture — that he saw on that first visit. He agreed to become a part of this enterprise, with the proviso that an acceptable model, in the spirit of Leonardo, had to be created. He didn't imagine himself to be an expert in the field, and he intended to listen closely to people he trusted.

"I give other people credit for giving me advice," he says, "and I give myself some credit for listening to them, for making sure their advice doesn't fall on deaf ears."

During the Meijer group's initial visit, Nina Akamu had been ordered by her employers not to speak with this potential savior of the project. Though she was known as one of the finest practitioners of *animaliere* sculpture in the United States, she was being treated as merely a hired hand. Her disappointment with the existing horse was well known to the LDVHI committee, who wanted to retain control and to minimize the spending of money that had been donated to them. Above all, the group wanted to retain Dent's horse, which meant a great deal to them emotionally.

By the Meijer team's second visit, however, Akamu met and spoke with everyone. She discovered that they agreed with her assessment of "Charlie's horse," and this gave her new energy in her campaign to create a completely new horse rather than continuing the attempt to fix the one at hand.

"LDVHI wanted to get the sculpture done," Akamu recalls, "give it to Italy, and be done with it. The Meijer perspective was very different: they wanted a high-quality work, and they did what they could to encourage that. There was so much pressure — for speed, for meeting deadlines — that when the Meijer team came in, we were looking forward to it days in advance, because it meant that the sense of pressure would be relieved. To see people who were enthusiastic, and who wanted to see the right changes made, was like a breath of fresh air."

One thing Akamu and others understood, which LDVHI's members had to

The group that called itself LDVHI (Leonardo Da Vinci's Horse, Incorporated) had built a certain measure of misunderstanding into its very name. It would come as no surprise, then, that Nina Akamu's eight-foot horse, which was to serve as the model for every other casting, was originally called "Leonardo da Vinci's Horse." That is what the Foundation had been publicizing and striving to create. Many people, including the sculptor, disliked that name, however. When David Hooker suggested that it be changed to something more suitable, Nina Akamu was happy to give it the far more honest (and accurate) name which it now bears: *Homage to Leonardo.*

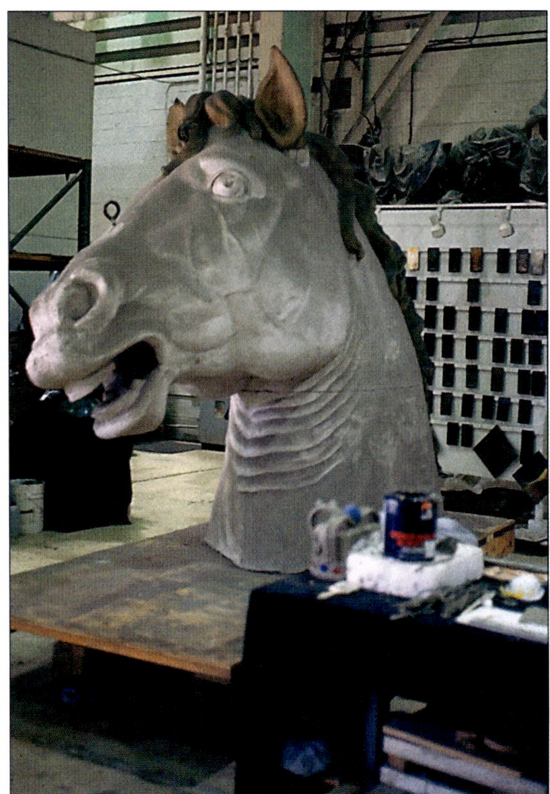

Head of Dent horse showing small ears, bulging eyes, inappropriate cheek veins, and grotesque mouth

Photo by Nina Akamu

learn, was that when you make a large model from a smaller one, any slight problem is magnified. In addition, you are now looking at it from far below, rather than straight on, and you see different things. It is partly a matter of perspective. This is something a classically trained sculptor would know, but that amateurs might not understand. The original horse was done by a group of amateurs. It didn't work at all. In addition to the other anatomical problems, the horse had a network of bulging veins in the face, and the chest and neck were all wrong when seen from below.

As it turned out, of course, Nina Akamu's horse was the one finally accepted, and Fred Meijer agreed to contribute funding that would enable the casting of two twenty-four-foot sculptures — one to be donated to the city of Milan, the other to be displayed at Meijer Gardens in Grand Rapids. Once again, however, we're getting ahead of the story.

At this point, LDVHI had raised more than a million dollars. But almost all of it had now been spent. It went toward creating Charlie Dent's eight-foot model, for enlarging it, for publicizing stories of the horse in the national media, for traveling to Italy to meet with Milanese officials, and for paying Akamu to "correct" the original problems. If that original horse were now to be destroyed, it would mean that there was nothing left. Nothing but the dream.

It is only natural that members of LDVHI resisted most of the changes and tried to retain "Charlie's horse" as long as possible.

"From where Nina and I were standing," recalls Glasson, "the problem was that we had to convince LDVHI to do a complete change, to start from scratch. From our standpoint it was necessary to start with Charlie's eight-foot model, make the necessary changes there, and use it to convince the committee that there was no choice: the Dent horse had to be destroyed."

Glasson created an advisory board of people from the National Sculpture Society, an association of elite figurative sculptors, and he used their support to help make the case. Much of the problem had to do with educating LDVHI members — convincing them that the head and the neck had to be in the correct position, that the legs needed to be properly placed, that the bones and muscles of the horse had to make anatomical sense. In addition, Akamu had to immerse herself in Leonardo's ideas, and in the sculptural traditions of his era, to bring something of his imagination to the resulting horse, which was, after all, supposed to be an *omaggio,* or homage, to Leonardo and the Renaissance.

"It was a very Machiavellian process that emerged," recalls Glasson. "There were a lot of special interests in this group, each working for their own ends. Sometimes out of ignorance, sometimes out of a desire for profit, sometimes out of other more personal or psychological motives. We had quite a time working around egos. The very carefully executed and thought-out process was developed by Rod Skidmore, Nina, myself, and others who were involved: it was a tremendous labyrinth."

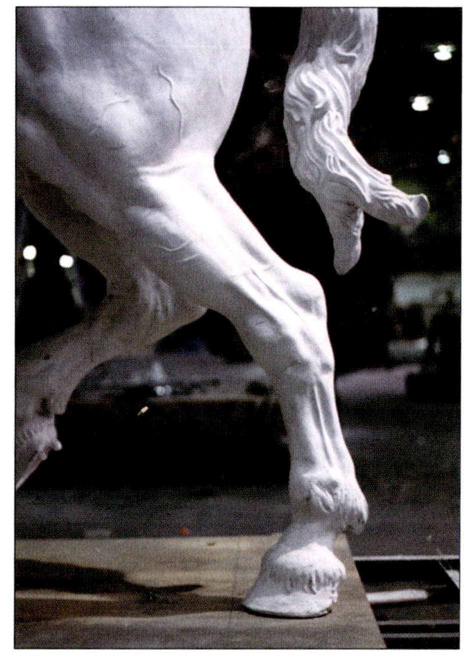

Forked tail Photo by Nina Akamu

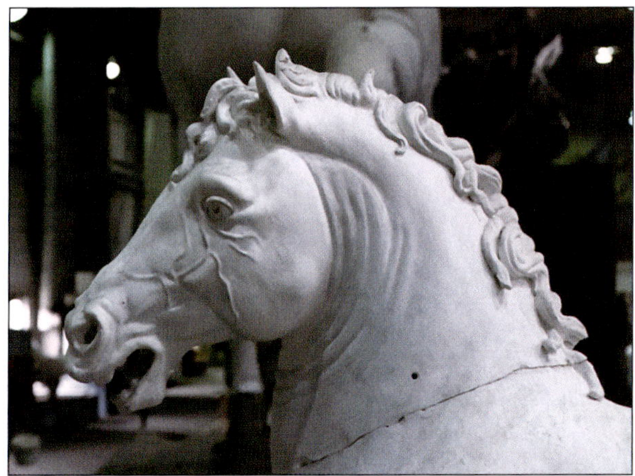

Head before corrections Photo by Nina Akamu

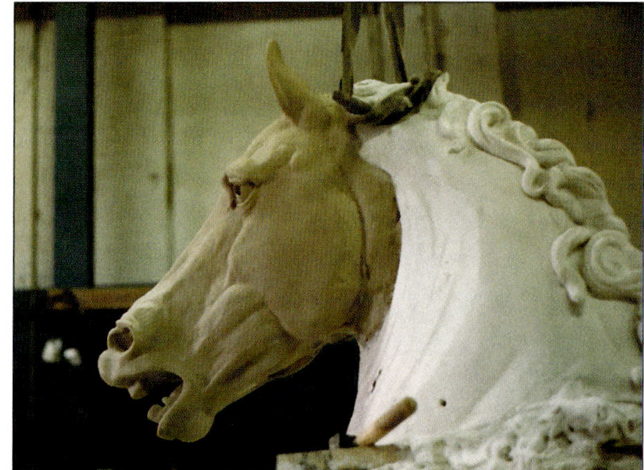

Head after corrections Photo by Nina Akamu

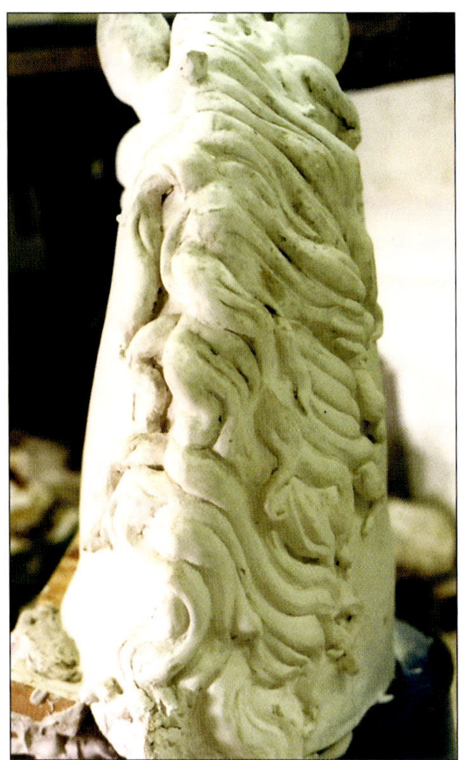

Dent horse's mane Photo by Nina Akamu

The horse's cheeks were too fat, so Akamu resculpted the entire head, eliminating the veins and repositioning the eyes. But then it became obvious that the rest of the horse was too fat. By the time she began thinning it down, the underlying problems with anatomy became even more glaring. Muscles had to be trimmed, the neck needed vertebral adjustment, and the angle of the head was too high, meaning that the face of a twenty-four-foot horse would be visible only to the birds overhead.

Ultimately, Charlie Dent's horse could not be saved. Rod Skidmore, as the project coordinator designated by LDVHI, had the important role of educating the committee, of weaning its members away from Charlie's horse.

As everyone came to understand, Dent had been the guru of LDVHI. Its members loved him: they had been captivated by his imagination and thus became fixated on the horse that had been created under his influence. They were in love with the old creature, and as Akamu made more and more corrections, there was finally nothing left of it but the mane.

"And they fought to keep the mane," she says, "even though it was little more than a collection of fat worms sliding along the neck." That fight wasn't successful either, but it was quite a struggle.

5. An Education

After Akamu finally convinced everyone that the Dent version of the sculpture had to be retired, and while she worked to complete her *Homage to Leonardo* at the Tallix foundry, Fred Meijer's appreciation for and understanding of sculpture underwent a tremendous transformation.

Quite a few highly regarded American sculptors were in the habit of casting their work at the Tallix foundry. There were notable public monuments, such as the FDR memorial mentioned in the *New York Times* article. But, perhaps more importantly for a sense of contemporary sculpture, a variety of illustrious sculptors would show up from time to time. During this period, for example, Claes Oldenburg was there working on a series of sculptures crafted to look like six-foot slices of blueberry pie. (Oldenburg, with his wife, Coosje van Bruggen, would eventually install their massive *Plantoir* at Meijer Gardens.)

Another icon of pop art, Roy Lichtenstein, had several pieces in progress. (Fred Meijer eventually acquired Lichtenstein's *Bonsai Tree*.) One of Alexander Liberman's massive steel constructions (*Aria,* now also in the collection of Meijer Gardens) had been disassembled and then put together again in the foundry yard, where it rose starkly against the industrial skyline of the town. Tom Otterness regularly cast his whimsical pieces there.

All in all, Fred Meijer learned a lot looking around the foundry yard. Many of the works he saw took an approach to artistic expression that he had not been exposed

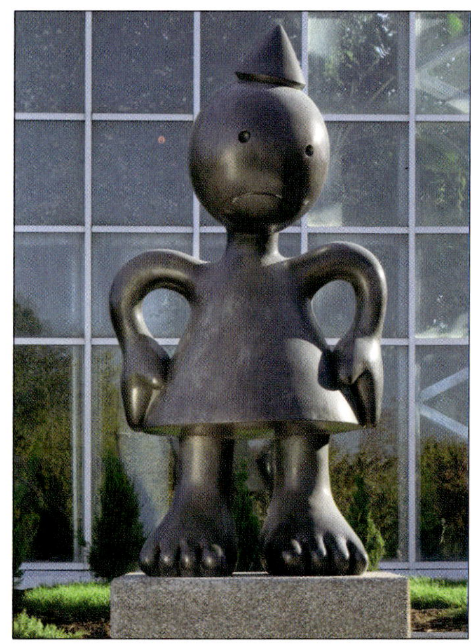

Tom Otterness. *Mad Mom,* 2001.

Photo by William J. Hebert

to before. He asked questions, pursued ideas about how to define art with anyone who would listen, and looked at sculpture (and the world) in new ways. He visited nearby Storm King, the vast sculpture park along the Hudson River whose collection outlines many trends in contemporary art. Tallix Foundry — and the surrounding region — was for several years a virtual school for sculpture for Fred Meijer.

It's a cliché to say, "I may not know much about art, but I know what I like." For most people, that's where it ends. What they know, and what they like, never changes. For Fred the real issue was to learn, to appreciate, and to enjoy art more widely and deeply than he had before. He embarked on his new curriculum with a passion.

As work on *The American Horse* progressed, it became clear to the Sculpture Advisory Committee that this component of Meijer Gardens was going to become far more important to the identity of the organization than the committee had previously imagined. Though he knew relatively little about sculpture when he began, Fred was willing to trust others who did know something about it. At the outset, his collection had only included figurative work: it was always clear what you were looking at. There was no room for ambiguity. He responded strongly to works that had narratives connected to them. He showed a preference for art that could be explained and discussed in clear, understandable terms.

An example of this aspect of his taste might be a suite of pieces by Kalamazoo sculptor Kirk Newman. After seeing some of Newman's work at a park in Kalamazoo, Fred arranged in the spring of 1996 to meet with the artist to discuss a possible commission.

"What I'd like to see," he explained over a cup of tea in Newman's living room, "is a work that shows children from every part of the world playing together. I'd like to see every racial or ethnic type that can be depicted in bronze. I'd like to show at least one child with an obvious physical handicap — using crutches or a wheel chair — and at least one child with Down syndrome. Can you do that?"

Newman thought that that would be a worthy subject. The two men talked about the scale of the statues, what kind of pedestals would work best, a schedule for completion, and possible pricing.

"How many children should I do?" asked Newman.

Meijer suggested that perhaps nine would be enough to cover all the qualities he wished to see.

Newman had another question: "More boys, or more girls?"

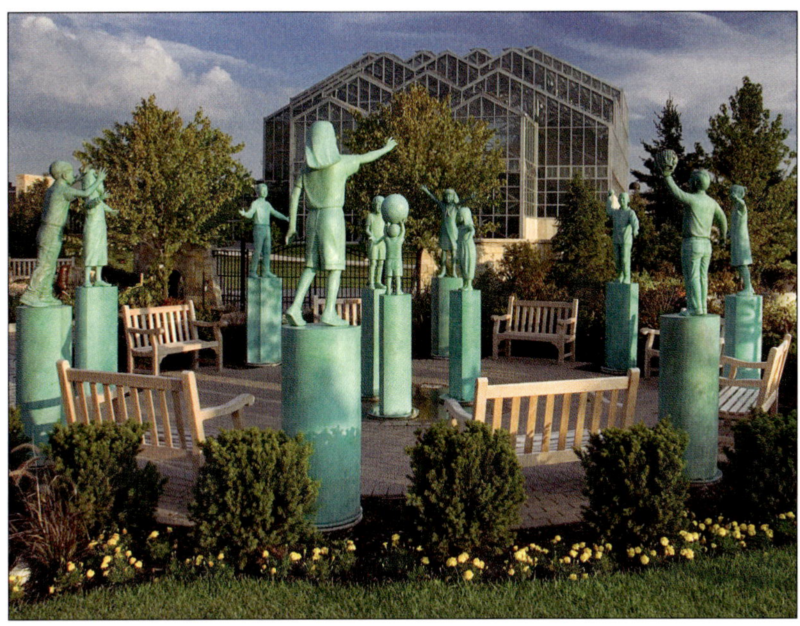

Kirk Newman. *Children of the World,* 1996. Photo by William J. Hebert

"Better make it ten," said his patron. "Five of each." And so it happened. Newman was invited to a corporate event in Grand Rapids, an occasion when many Meijer associates brought their children to a picnic, and he began to sketch then and there.

Before long, Newman's *Children of the World* stood in a prominent position out front at Meijer Gardens, next to the Leslie Tassel English Perennial Garden. It was one of the first things people saw as they approached the building. The work was later moved to the Lena Meijer Children's Garden, where it gained an eleventh child (on permanent loan from the collection of Grand Valley State University), and where, joined with a splashing fountain, it continues to attract viewers and tempts children to get their feet wet on the hot days of summer.

Well before *The American Horse* was finished, a process that took nearly four years, Fred had decided to purchase Alexander Liberman's *Aria,* the 55-foot-tall

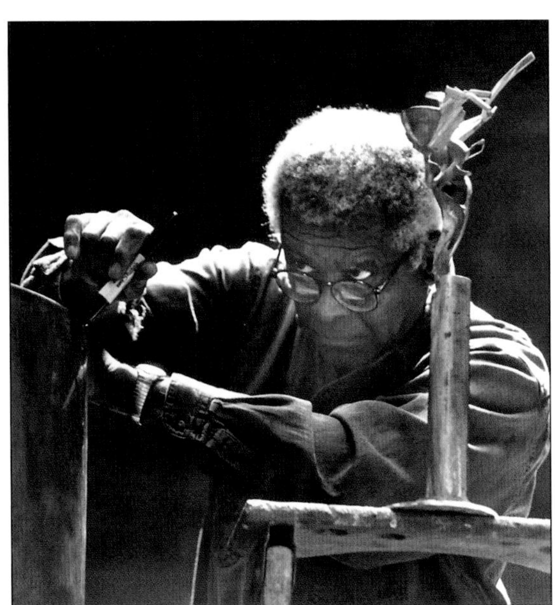

Richard Hunt at work on *Column of the Free Spirit*

abstract sculpture he'd seen at Tallix. Shortly thereafter, he approved a commission for Richard Hunt's *Column of the Free Spirit.* These pieces represented a significant development in Fred Meijer's taste. They were abstractions, whose physical shape was not based on anything in nature.

If the sculpture committee talked to Fred about acquiring a work that he didn't like or didn't understand on first viewing, he was open-minded and willing to learn more. He would ask questions, seek additional information, and, soon thereafter, would find himself moving in new directions. He was further encouraged by discussions among board members and sculpture committee members as they met and traveled.

On one occasion, for example, while the sculpture committee was visiting the Walker Art Center in Minneapolis, Bill Padnos, a longtime member of the committee, got into a discussion with Fred over lunch in the museum's café. Padnos focused on how to accommodate various levels of taste and sophistication when establishing a public art collection. He used the analogy of a library, suggesting that Meijer Gardens could create a visual library, where not all the "books" will suit any one person's tastes or interests but where each person could find something to enjoy. Meijer found the analogy apt, and it helped put the future of Meijer Gardens' collection into perspective.

During a visit to the Walker, Fred encountered one of Deborah Butterfield's horses on display at the adjacent Minneapolis Sculpture Garden. Soon afterward, Fred and Lena Meijer arranged to visit Butterfield in her studio, where they made arrangements to acquire yet another horse, Butterfield's *Cabin Creek,* now grazing in a field not far from *The American Horse.*

It has been this quality of openness and curiosity on Fred's part, in addition to his energy and his financial support, that have made Meijer Gardens such a success, not only in sculpture, but as a broadly based cultural institution.

By now it was clear to everyone that there would be many more acquisitions following on the heels of the horse, and, if the growth of a collection was to be carefully managed, a curator would be needed. The Sculpture Advisory Committee began to discuss the need for a curator of sculpture, and in short order Fred agreed that such a position was necessary.

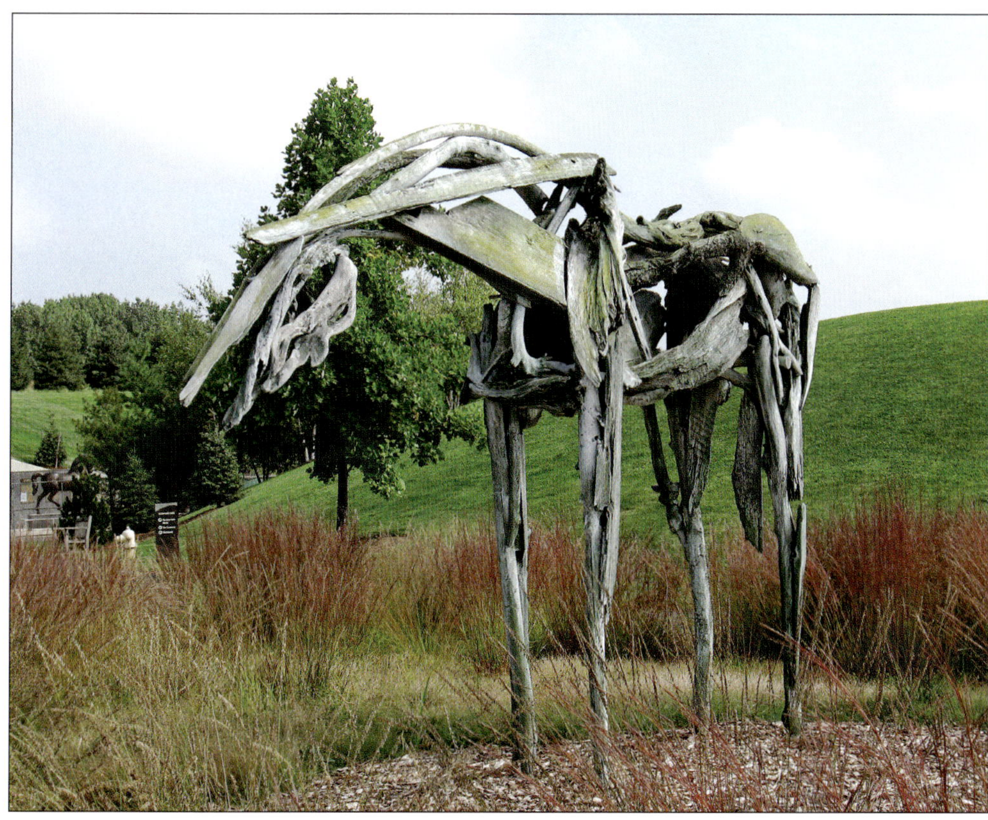

Deborah Butterfield. *Cabin Creek,* 1999. Photo by Larry ten Harmsel

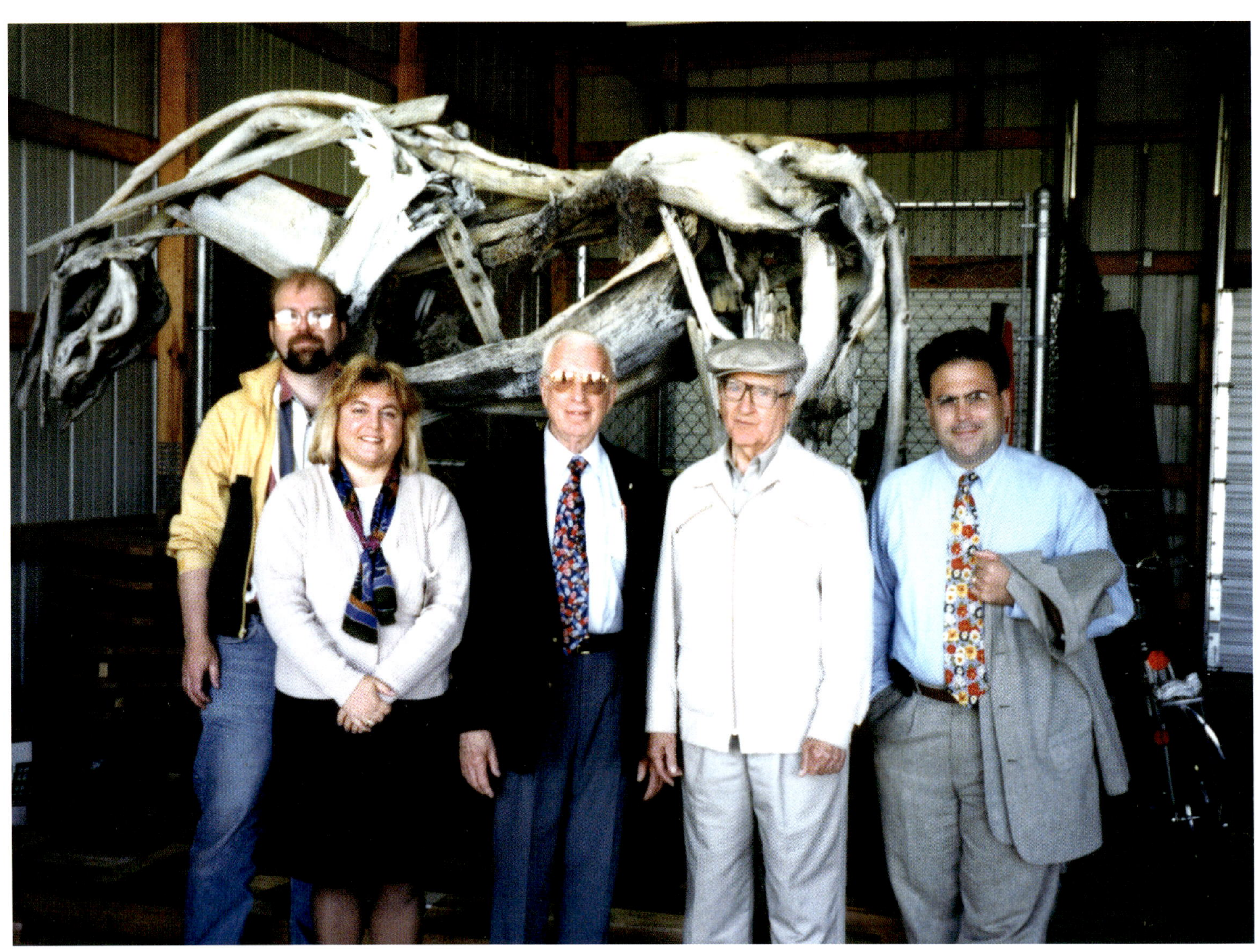

Caleb Brennan, Julie Dreyer, Fred Meijer, Herman van Nijverdal, and Joe Becherer in front of newly acquired *Cabin Creek*, 1999

6. A Curatorial Vision

Joseph Antenucci Becherer, an art historian with degrees from Ohio University and Indiana University, was a young college administrator and professor, and had recently curated an important exhibition for the Grand Rapids Art Museum. This project brought the works of Pietro Perugino, who had been teacher and mentor of the Renaissance painter Raphael Sanzio, to Grand Rapids.

It was the largest exhibition ever of Perugino's paintings, and the first in North America. It was also the first national show organized and situated in Grand Rapids, an idea Becherer developed out of the sister-city relationship between Grand Rapids and Perugia, Perugino's home town.

"I like to think the project served as a kind of cultural awakening for the city," says Becherer, "as well as being a shot in the arm for the Art Museum. There hadn't been anything of similar proportions on the art scene since the installation of the Calder stabile in 1969." Becherer served as liaison with curators in Perugia and elsewhere, and was involved in all aspects of the event, which garnered international attention. Before long, his name was being mentioned, privately, as a possible candidate for what would be a new job at Meijer Gardens. As yet, he had no idea.

He recalls hearing about *The American Horse* around the time the Perugino exhibition was finishing up. There was a sort of murmur around town, and he became vaguely aware of it. "Such a big-name artist always creates a stir," he adds. "Lots of people would mention it to me, because Leonardo was an exact contemporary of Perugino. Other than an art-historical awareness, I knew very little about the project.

"Hank Meijer, who I came to know while we were working together on the Maya Lin commission for the city, invited me to lunch a couple of times to talk about it. We met at One Trick Pony or the Cottage Bar, one of those places close to Monument Park, because it was convenient for me. He started explaining something about the project and his father's involvement. He didn't really go into the aesthetics, but wanted to talk about the historical setting. We had some really enjoyable conversations, which wouldn't have been a part of our normal work life."

Becherer was asked to come along to the Tallix Foundry on several occasions, beginning around the time that the original Dent horse had been rejected. Going to Nina Akamu's work space, he found himself reassured by the variety of images she had there as sources of inspiration. It put his mind at ease about the quality of the work she was likely to produce. He could see she had done a serious job of research, and was looking at a much bigger picture of how the Renaissance depicted horses, not simply enslaving herself to a few Leonardo sketches.

"You can't take something the size of a postage stamp and render it at 24 feet," he insists. But Akamu's wall was festooned with Leonardo studies, Verrocchio studies, images of master drawings from the Albertina Museum in Vienna, copies of Velasquez equestrian paintings, and so forth. She had lived and worked in Italy for ten years. She had ridden Iberian horses. Clearly, she knew her stuff.

"I had a lot of heated discussions with people," Becherer recalls, "about the extent to which we could associate the name of Leonardo with the horse — I thought it crucial to connect the work with Nina, not so much with Leonardo. I didn't want to deceive people by suggesting that with a wave of a wand and some fairy dust this was going to be Leonardo's 500-year-old object being brought back to life. You had to talk about what it truly was, and credit Nina as the sculptor, talking about her as someone who used Leonardo as an intellectual springboard for her own concepts."

As the horse neared completion, the issue of finding a curator grew more important. Now almost everyone was looking beyond the horse to what might happen next.

On April 13, 1999, Becherer was asked to lunch with Brent Dennis, Meijer Gardens' Executive Director.

"I thought it was for lunch," he remembers. "We sat in the café, and Brent was there, along with Fred and Lena Meijer, and Earl Holton. We said very little about what I had thought would be the subject."

Fred began to talk, slowly, about his interest in sculpture. By this time he had begun to recognize the limitations of his existing collection and was determined to develop it further. He had visited the Kröller-Müller Museum in the Netherlands and had explored other European sculpture collections. He shared a dream about the idyllic possibilities of creating a world-class sculpture park in Grand Rapids. He reminisced about his childhood. Becherer listened in silence. He had not imagined things would go in this direction.

By then the sculpture committee had reiterated that a more concerted professional approach was needed to bring Fred's ideas into shape, but it was difficult for anyone to come to terms with the task. There wasn't a clear idea of the direction things would take. And yet there was also a sense of urgency. The new phase of construction, just being completed, included a gallery, but there was no one on the staff with gallery experience.

As the minutes rolled by, Earl and Fred, and sometimes Brent Dennis, "started

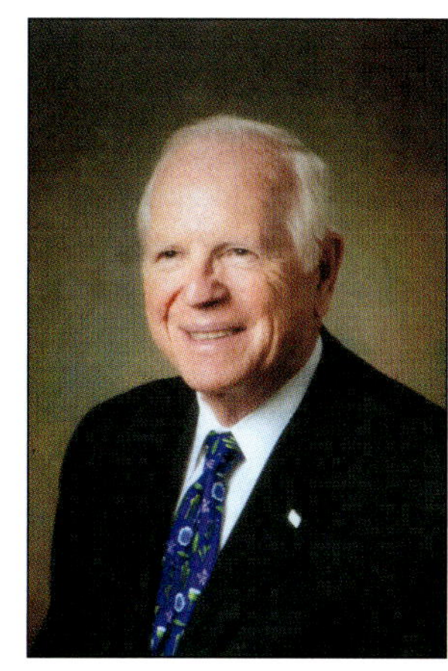

Earl Holton, president of Meijer, Inc., from 1980 to 1998, served as chairman of the capital campaign that raised the funds for Frederik Meijer Gardens & Sculpture Park. A close friend and colleague of Fred for more than fifty years, he has helped oversee the organization of Meijer Gardens since its inception.

asking me these questions about collecting, and use of spaces, and all sorts of very specific, detailed issues.

"I said, 'Are you asking for my opinion, or are you interviewing me?' I'm a little embarrassed now about how forthright I was."

What developed was a clear sense of personal confidence. Fred respected Becherer's expertise and commitment, and Becherer trusted Fred's determination. "This," he sensed, "is a man of his word."

After lunch, when his wife Lisa picked him up, she looked at him and said, "What happened to you? Are you okay?"

He hadn't spoken a word, but he must have looked a bit shaken. Finally, he admitted it. "I think I've just been offered a job," he said.

In August of 1999, after negotiations that included creating an academic chair for him at Aquinas College, Becherer accepted the position of Curator of Sculpture at Meijer Gardens and began the process of shaping its future.

His first task, in the fall of that year, was to clarify a vision about what was necessary to build a world-class collection. He asked the Sculpture Advisory Committee to help compile a master list of Modern and Contemporary sculptors, from the late nineteenth century to the present. This list provided a guide and a database for possible acquisitions of sculpture, and it established the direction in which the collection would grow.

He also helped create an ambitious program of sculpture exhibitions, reinforcing the educational and aesthetic goals of Meijer Gardens.

Caleb Brennan, a sculptor and part-time employee, was hired as assistant curator for collections. Becherer then hired Laurene Grunwald as assistant curator for exhibitions. Both helped with the complex issues surrounding the acquisition, installation, and management of collections and exhibitions, which would grow to national and international prominence in the coming years. As the program rapidly grew, it needed additional expertise. Marlene Vanderhill and Jennifer Flanders were hired in the fledgling Sculpture Department, and Linda Thompson and Heidi Holst, both art historians, took leadership positions in the Education Department.

In August, Meijer Gardens unveiled Deborah Butterfield's *Cabin Creek*, an utterly contemporary form of equine sculpture. October saw the acquisition of Magdalena Abakanowicz's powerful, painful *Figure on a Bench*. In January of 2000, after Fred had come to know and like Arnaldo Pomodoro, Meijer Gardens acquired the Italian artist's mathematical abstraction, *Disk in the Form of a Desert Rose*. These three works, acquired within a few months of Becherer's arrival on the scene, helped to consolidate an expanding curatorial vision and set the stage for further institutional growth.

7. Work Continues

Once the decision had been made to scrap Dent's horse, Nina Akamu was no longer an anonymous ghost sculptor. Suddenly she became artist in residence at Tallix, working in a studio in one of the outbuildings of the foundry. It meant her days were much longer, and in some ways she was under more pressure than she had been before.

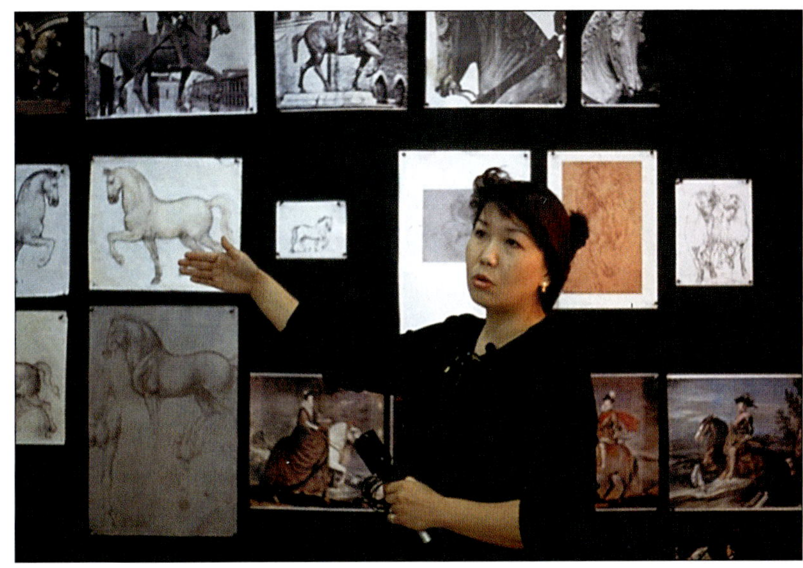

Akamu with bulletin board

She had to start from scratch. She worked from a variety of sketches and studies Leonardo had made, plus whatever she could cobble together from her own study of Renaissance sculpture, her years of living in Italy and working in the artists' enclave of Pietrasanta, and her developing awareness of the shape she wanted to see emerge. There was nothing definitive to give her direction; she had to discover her own sense of what she was after.

The project was slated to be finished by late summer of 1999, five hundred years after the destruction of Leonardo's clay model in Milan. That deadline had been agreed on for both large castings, the one going to Milan and the one going to Michigan. Sponsors had been lined up, and extensive plans were under way. The calendar was unforgiving, and it was full. Time constraints meant that Akamu had no chance to make a small model and then gradually work her way up to the larger scale. Nearly a year had been wasted already. She began immediately with an eight-foot master model to be used for all subsequent castings.

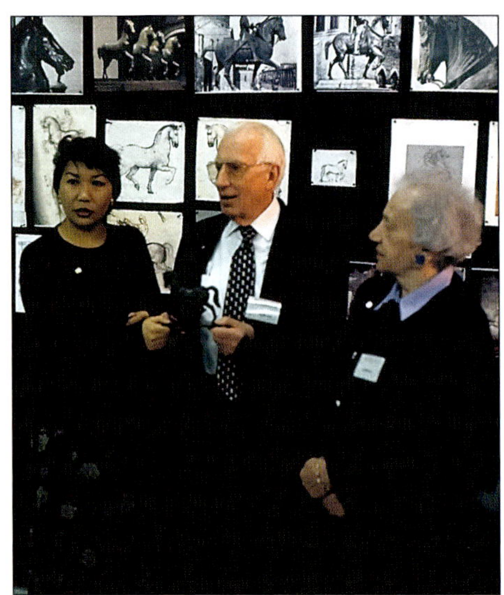

Akamu with Fred and Lena Meijer

It had to be precisely calibrated, since any flaws would be fatally magnified when the eight-foot version was increased to its eventual twenty-four-foot height. Three times as tall meant nine times as massive. With so much at stake in these dimensions, everything she did had to be exact.

In reality, Nina was much more prepared for the job ahead than even she knew. She had spent months studying Leonardo's work and familiarizing herself with equine anatomy. She understood the environment in which she would need to work. She was becoming more aware of the different parties involved, and of the personalities that had to be accommodated. By this time she also had a better understanding of the materials and the foundry processes. She had integrated these elements and was working carefully with all of them. There was enormous pressure, but somehow everything was moving along.

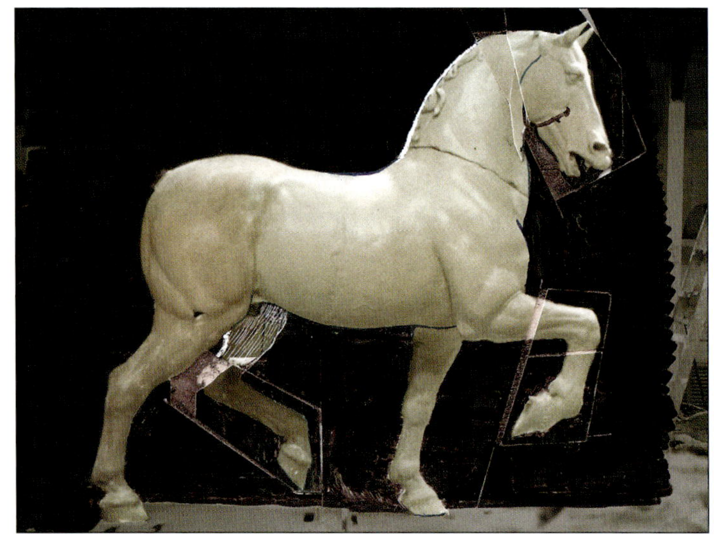

Akamu Collage Photo by Nina Akamu

"Sometime during all of this chaos," Akamu recalls, "I made a rough collage. After studying Leonardo's drawings in more detail and making lots of meticulous calculations, I had formed a pretty good 3-D image in my mind. I created the collage from small photos, black marker, and tape. This was definitely a pre-computer image. I didn't own a computer then, much less know how to use one."

The resulting collaged image, though crude, was effective. Akamu submitted her patchwork to the board of LDVHI for approval. Although she'd had many disagreements with some members of the board, they, too, were feeling the pressure of time. They understood that Akamu was their only chance to complete the project. They couldn't turn her down.

"At that moment," she says, "I remember thinking, 'Omigosh, Nina, what have you gotten yourself into?' I was so naïve. It was just the beginning."

From that moment, however, things started moving swiftly. No longer was she programming changes into a flawed template; with the general approval of the committee, she could pursue her goal single-mindedly.

Within a year, an eight-foot model in clay was ready for casting. Everyone now involved with the increasingly complicated process approved of *Homage to Leonardo,* which is what Nina eventually named the master model. Finally, a year and a half after Nina Akamu's initial involvement, a cast was made.

When "Homage" emerged from the molds, foundry workers carefully sandblasted it, leaving it with a silvery hue. Eventually, they applied a dark brown patina, using a chemical process that involved reheating the surface. Then the real work began. In less than a year this massive project had to be finished.

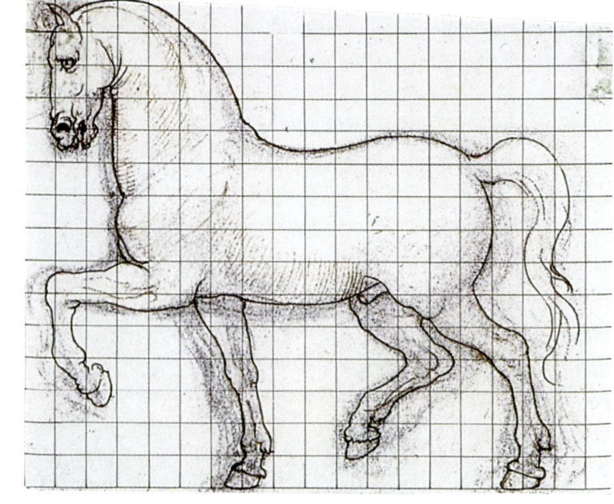

Master sketch Photo by Nina Akamu

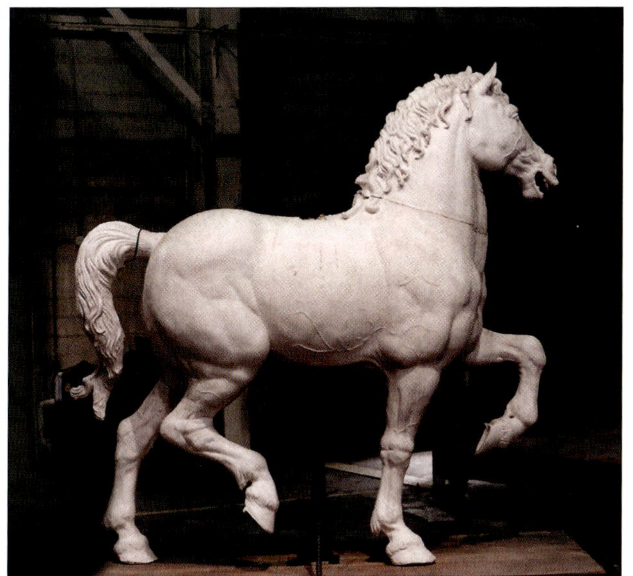

Original Dent horse

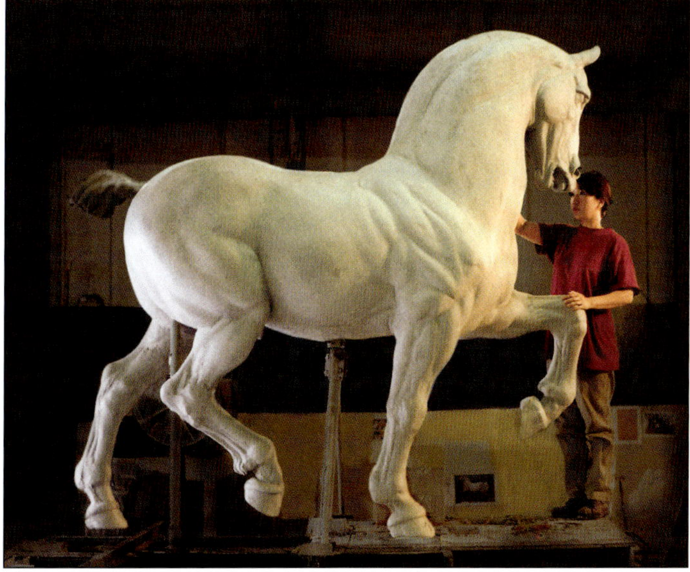

Akamu's studio horse

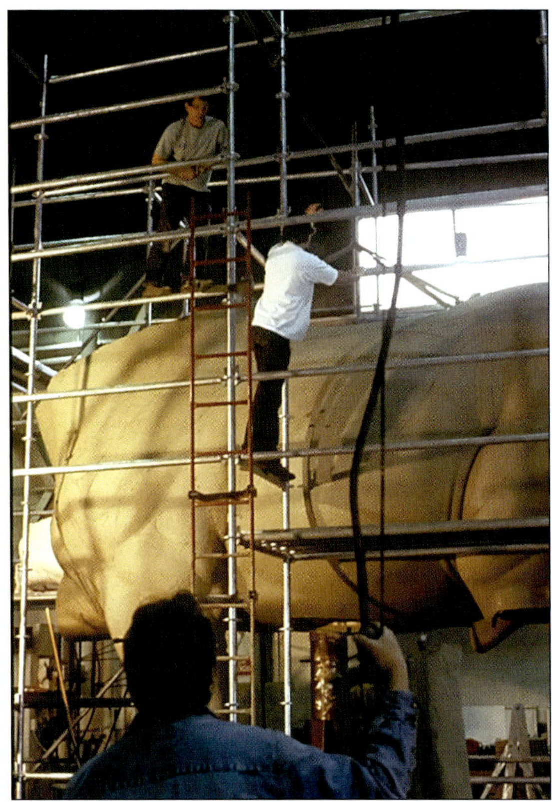

Scaffolding Photo by Larry ten Harmsel

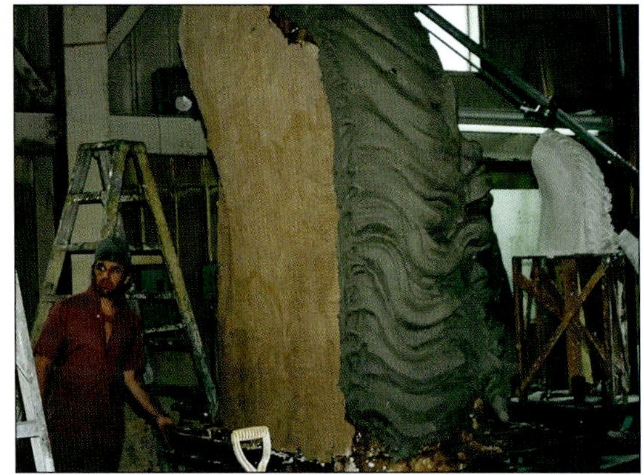

Mane enlargement Photo by Larry ten Harmsel

Using an enlargement tool, a mechanical arm called a pantograph, Akamu and foundry workers began constructing a twenty-four-foot clay model. Although mechanical assistance works well to create the basic shapes of a smaller object on a larger scale, it does not effectively capture the details and textures that are crucial to successful enlarging. For that, the artist had to work every inch of the new surface herself. It quickly became apparent to Akamu that she would need skilled assistants.

Within weeks, seven assistants, elite and carefully trained sculpture students at art schools in the New York area, were hired to work in the foundry. Supported by scaffolding, and often strapped into position, they clambered over the surface of the emerging clay horse like mountain climbers exploring new terrain.

Akamu oversaw their work, sometimes joining them on the scaffolds, but more often directing their efforts from below. Using a laser pointer, she developed a system of communication that allowed her to engage in extremely precise close-up manipulation of the soft clay, while standing at a distance that allowed her to see things in the necessary perspective.

Each day saw progress as the sculptor and the seven assistants worked away. Every week saw another milestone. The tight schedule dictated how much time could be spent on particular areas of the enlargement: a week to work on the shoulder muscles, a day apiece on the four hooves, a week on the head, and so forth. Now and then something went disastrously wrong. One day, as workers prepared to move the seven-foot-tall head, delicately molded in soft green clay, the heavy nylon support strap broke under the weight, and the head fell twenty feet. There was a loud noise, then a softer thud, and suddenly nothing remained but a misshapen lump of green on the foundry floor. An additional week had to be spent reworking the head, paid for by insurance. But there was no insurance on the calendar's steady march. Deadlines had to be met.

And then one day the clay enlargement was finished. It dominated the cavernous space of the foundry, dwarfing the people who strolled by. By now the horse was attracting a good deal of media attention. Akamu remembers how pleased she was by the look of the enlarged horse.

Then came the next stage. It had to be disassembled once again, sliced into fifty-two pieces of a size that allowed for casting, and outlined with heavy aluminum foil. The expense and uncertainty of casting it the way Leonardo had specified — as a solid mass of bronze — was never considered. When finished, this horse would be almost a featherweight, a hollow shell, a mere ten tons of artfully constructed bronze.

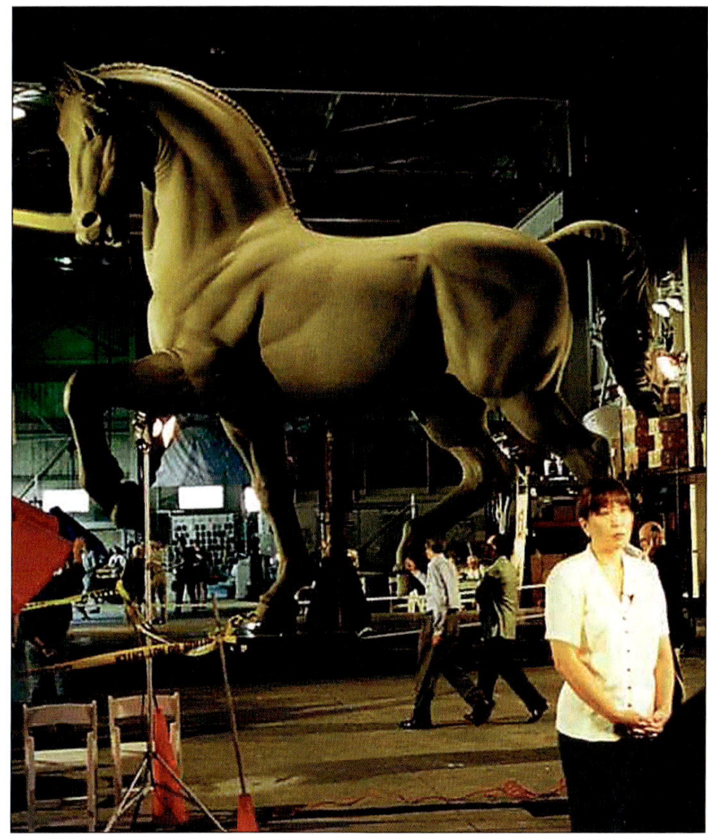

Akamu and clay model Photo by Dave Meinke

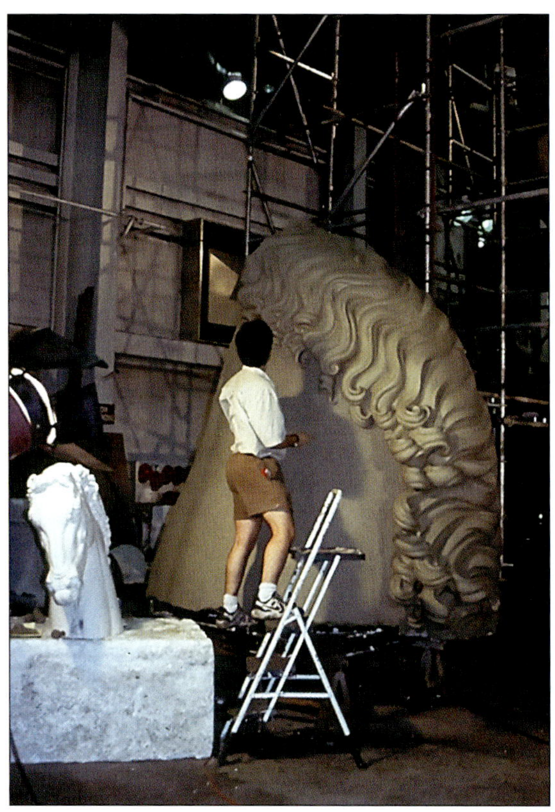

Finishing touches Photo by Larry ten Harmsel

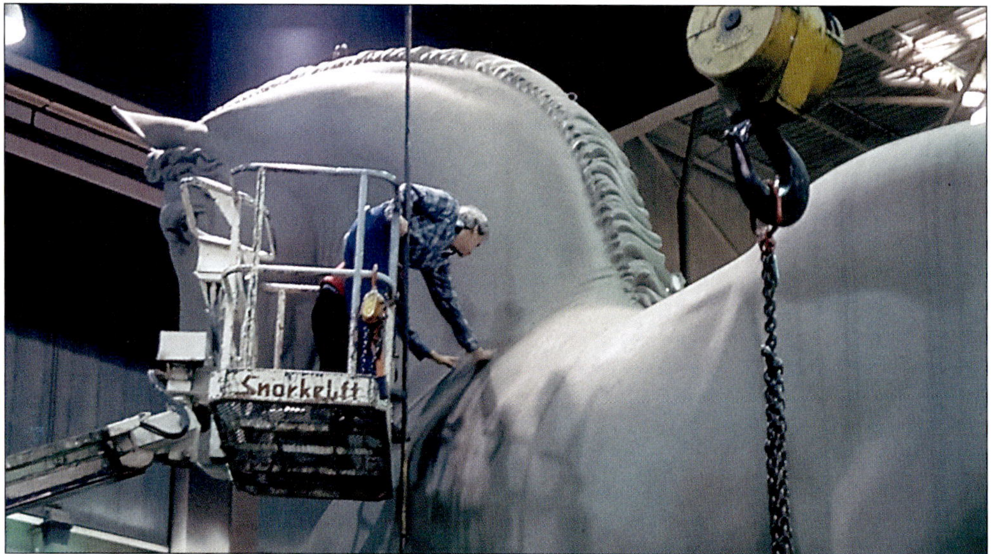

Surface touches Photo by Larry ten Harmsel

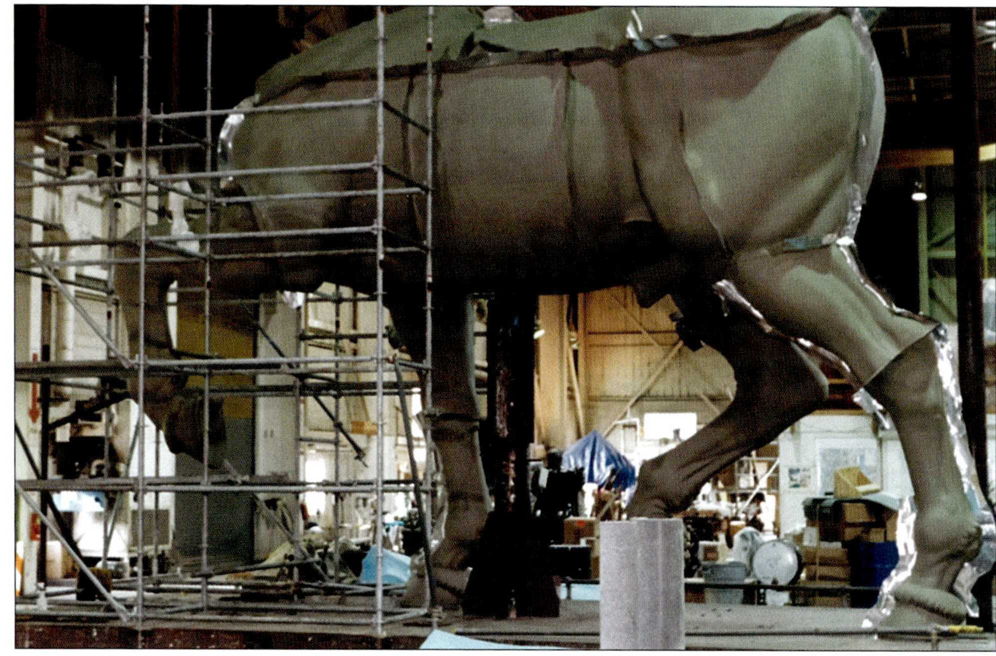

Preparations for casting Photo by Larry ten Harmsel

8. Whose Is It?

At this point, so far into the project that they were within sight of completion, major problems having nothing to do with the physical horse arose. One was about the recognition of Nina Akamu's position as artist. Because the original Dent horse had been completely discarded, from its grimacing head to its forking tail, this new horse could not in any sense be called Dent's. Yet that is just what the LDVHI was doing in its publicity releases. Nina addressed her concerns in a formal letter, which she sent to the committee on November 12, 1998.

In the letter she reminds the members that they had signed an affidavit recognizing the horse as solely a product of Akamu's "creative efforts, judgments, and original designs." Yet they were now claiming otherwise. Akamu had other problems, too, which she details in the letter:

> *Such statements as:*
>
> 1. *We are recreating Leonardo's masterpiece;*
> 2. *We are finishing his sculpture for him;*
> 3. *We are following his drawings as closely as possible;*
> 4. *It is a Renaissance horse;*
> 5. *Leonardo would have been proud.*
>
> *Such statements are not only unrealistic but harmful.*

These claims had been made in various news releases that the LDVHI was sending out to the national press. They were all false, of course, but they attracted a great deal of attention. Akamu suggested that the committee was being "unrealistic, naïve, presumptuous, and unconscionably conceited," and that such statements, if they continued, could discredit the entire process in the minds of knowledgeable people in Italy and in the United States.

At about that same time another obstacle arose. It had been ignored or glossed over for months, but now it required a period of intense negotiation and teams of contending lawyers. Fred Meijer's donation had been intended for two purposes: to help defray the cost of the gift horse for Milan and to pay for another casting that would be installed in Grand Rapids. Initially, LDVHI had stipulated that the Meijer Gardens casting (now formally called *The American Horse*) would be twenty-one feet tall, in contrast to the twenty-four-foot Italian horse.

Well into the process of enlargement, that assumption continued to hold. Newspaper articles from 1998 invariably refer to a twenty-one-foot horse coming to Grand Rapids. But executives at the foundry had been watching Akamu's team: eight people working at peak efficiency. By now they had developed a clear idea of the expense, time, and effort that went into an enlargement. They began to realize that it was logistically impossible to create a twenty-one-foot casting within the budget — and on schedule.

Far better, they decided, to make two identical castings. In that way the quality would be assured, expenses could be held in line, and deadlines could be met, both in Italy and in the United States. A few people from the Meijer organization flew to Italy immediately to discuss this new possibility with Milanese cultural representatives. It required some delicate maneuvering, but eventually the Italians agreed that it would be fine, from their point of view, for *The American Horse* to be the same size as *Il Cavallo,* as it is called in Milan. Their only condition, articulated by spokesperson Emilio Iaia, was that Meijer Gardens mount the horse at ground level, while it would perch on a pedestal in Italy. Since people at Meijer Gardens had already decided to display the horse at ground level, this was no concession at all.

However, according to American intellectual-property law, LDVHI owned the rights to the entire process. These rights were later transferred to Frederik Meijer Gardens & Sculpture Park, but LDVHI still owned them at this time. A slight majority of the LDVHI committee decided, for symbolic and personal reasons, that *The American Horse* should be smaller than the one given to Italy. A series of intense legal negotiations instantly erupted: pages were scribbled full of notes, tempers flared, more pages of legalese emerged, and more disagreements ensued.

LDVHI was in a peculiar position: although it owned the rights, it did not have the money to create both a twenty-four-foot and a twenty-one-foot horse, and what money it had left (much of which had come from Meijer in the first place) was now being drained by legal fees. In a last-ditch effort to reach a compromise, the committee agreed to let the foundry cast two identical horses. However, it then asked that the horseshoes be filed off the hooves of *The American Horse,* which would make it a few inches shorter than *Il Cavallo.* Greg Glasson, the former president of Tallix, remembers this request as a nearly comical event. The foundry would never agree to deface one of its own products, he said. That proposal died quickly, and a final agreement was settled on in the terms outlined earlier by Emilio Iaia.

When a newspaper reporter later asked Fred Meijer about the legal dustup, he downplayed the disagreements. "When a baby is born," he said, "there might be a lot of labor pains. There might even be blood. But after things have calmed down, what you say is, 'Hey, this is a beautiful baby.'"

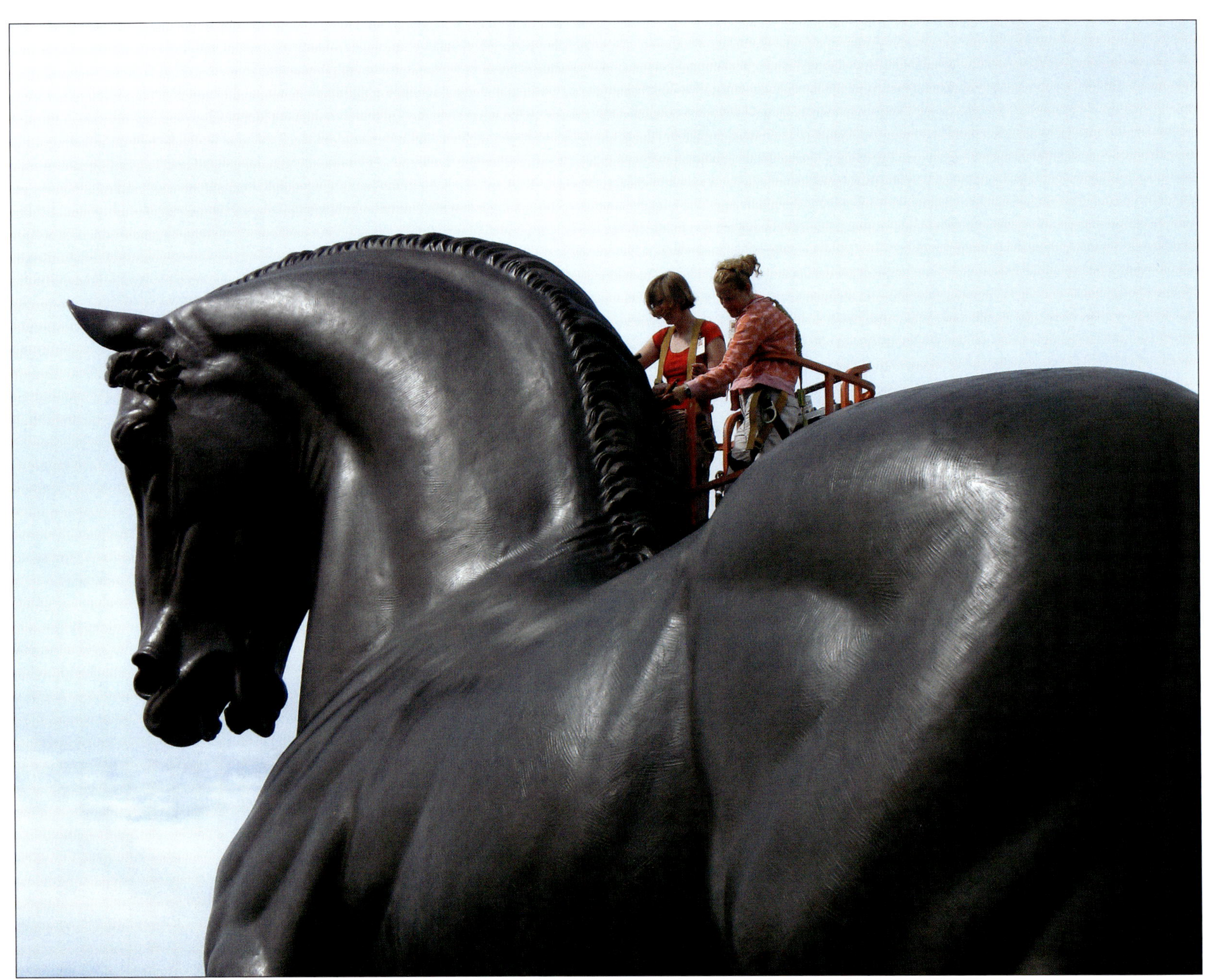

Laurene Grunwald and Jennie Flanders during yearly cleaning

9. Nearly Done

The last stage could finally begin. The bronze used in both castings of the giant horse was donated by the Louis Padnos Iron and Metal Company in Holland, Michigan. The precise composition of the alloy was determined by the foundry, of course, but much of the copper — the major ingredient — came from the recycled radiators of Michigan automobiles, making *The American Horse* an industrial example of the metaphorical "beating swords into plowshares." Once the ingots arrived, the forges were fired up.

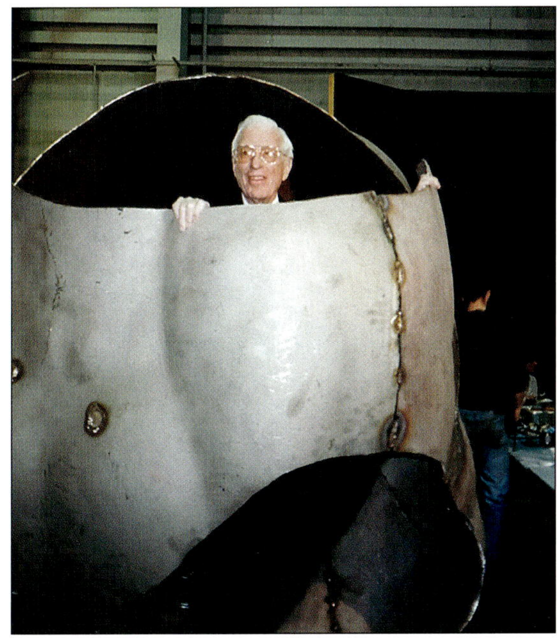

Fred Meijer in torso Photo by Larry ten Harmsel

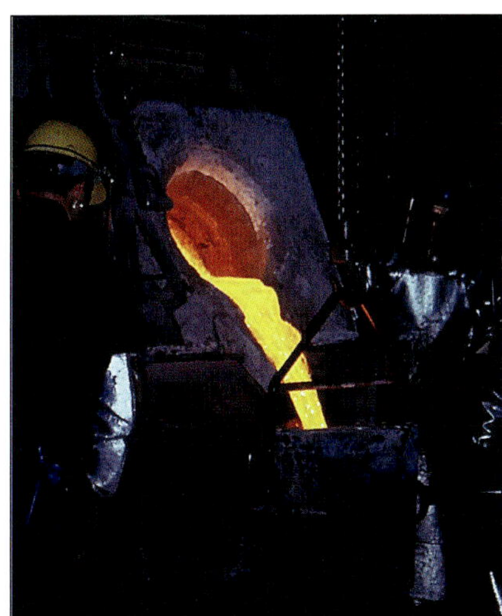

Molten bronze Photo by Larry ten Harmsel

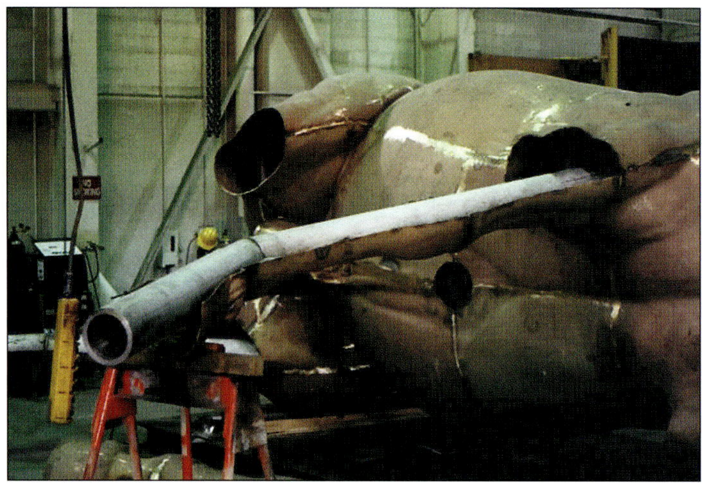

Armature Photo by Larry ten Harmsel

Over the ensuing weeks, 104 carefully modeled pieces of bronze (fifty-two for each horse) sat cooling on the floor. These pieces, mapped and numbered, were spot-welded into place. Large segments of the twin horses lay on the foundry floor, awaiting the next steps: more welding, more scaffolding, the insertion of a carefully engineered stainless steel armature, and more surface work by Akamu and her team.

Eventually two giant horses stood side by side, ready to be patinated in a rich brown finish.

As a final touch, after everything else was completed, Akamu etched the name of Leonardo into the right eye of the horse; she etched Charles Dent's name into the left eye. Those inscriptions are not visible to anyone on the ground, and have no effect on the composition in any way, except to complete the act of homage to the genius whose imagination had provided the inspiration for this lengthy creative process, and to the American pilot who was its cheerleader.

One of the twins was then brought outside the foundry walls for passersby to see. Crowds gathered, and traffic clogged the narrow streets of Beacon, New York. NBC sent its correspondent Rehema Ellis to report on the event for the *Today Show.*

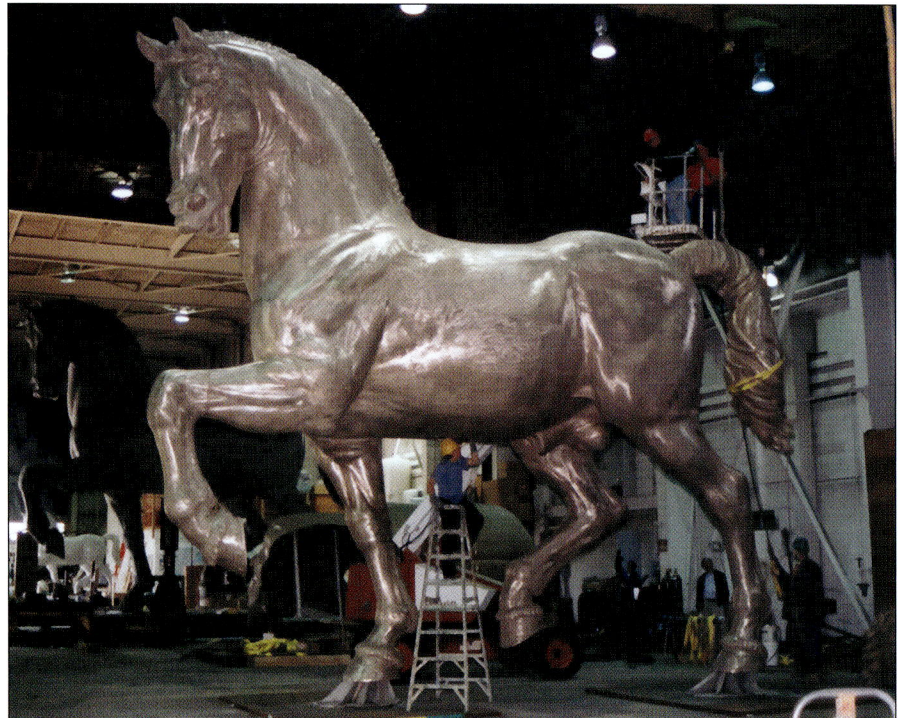

After sandblasting, before patination Photo by Dave Meinke

After years of work, months of negotiations, endless days and hours of endeavor, the horses were finally ready to be shipped to their far-off destinations — one to the east, one to the west. Of course, such large objects could not fit into a plane or a truck, so once again they were sliced into pieces. This time there were fewer pieces — four legs, a tail, a trunk, and a massive neck and head. One set was flown to Italy, while the other set was loaded onto semitrailers and hauled to Grand Rapids. *Smithsonian* magazine featured the story on its cover in September 1998.

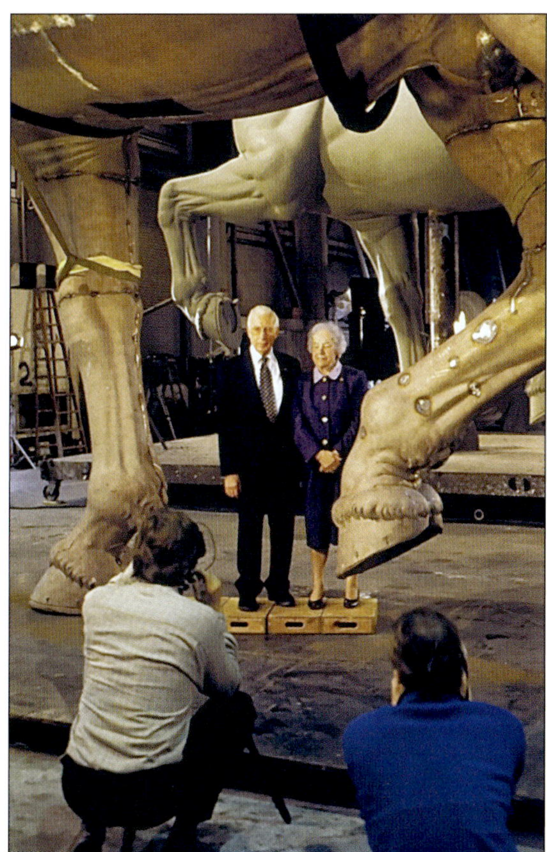

Fred and Lena at foundry Photo by Dave Meinke

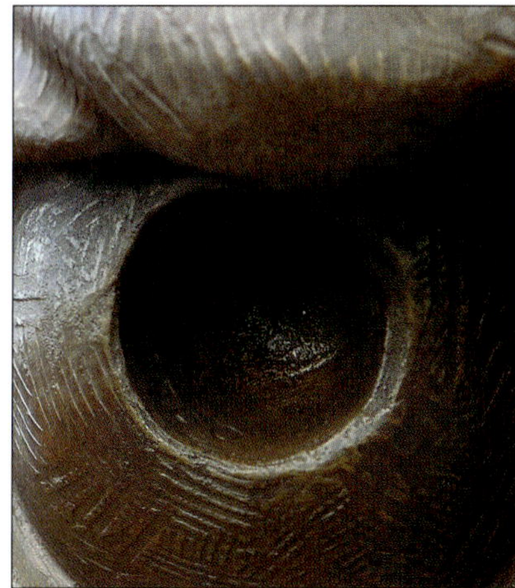

Right eye, inscribed "LEONARDO" ("RDO" visible) Photo by Dave Meinke

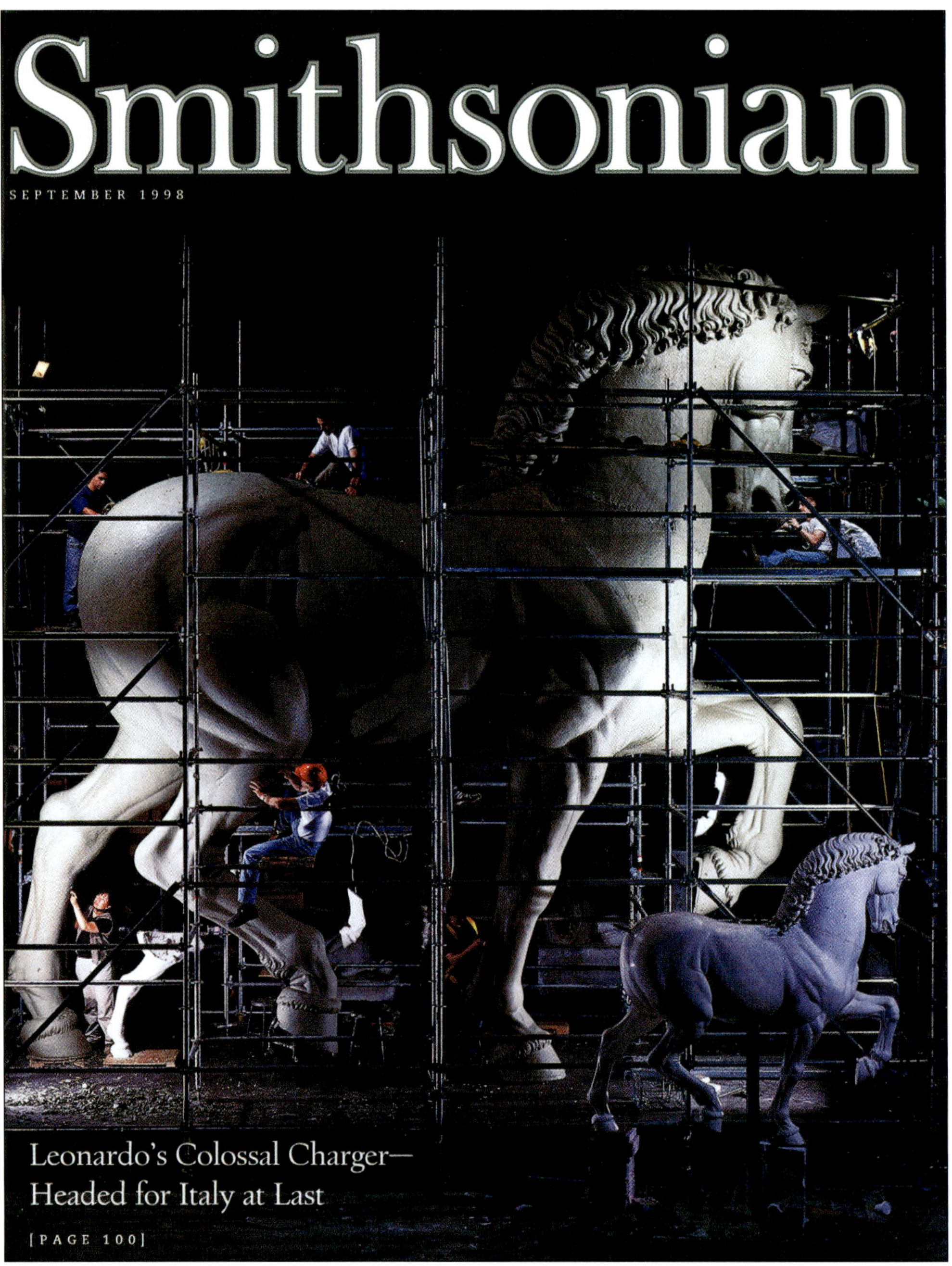

"A Long Shot Pays Off," *Smithsonian Magazine*, September 1998. Cover image used by permission.

10. Preparing the Ground

A Grand Rapids design firm, Progressive Engineering, had helped develop and mold the landscape of Meijer Gardens. Darwin Feuerstein, a landscape architect and designer with Progressive, took primary responsibility for creating a space to hold the massive *American Horse*. After extensive discussions with the staff and the Sculpture Advisory Committee, he settled on a sloping four-acre field just north of the conservatory. Unfortunately, whenever it rained, that field became a morass of slippery clay.

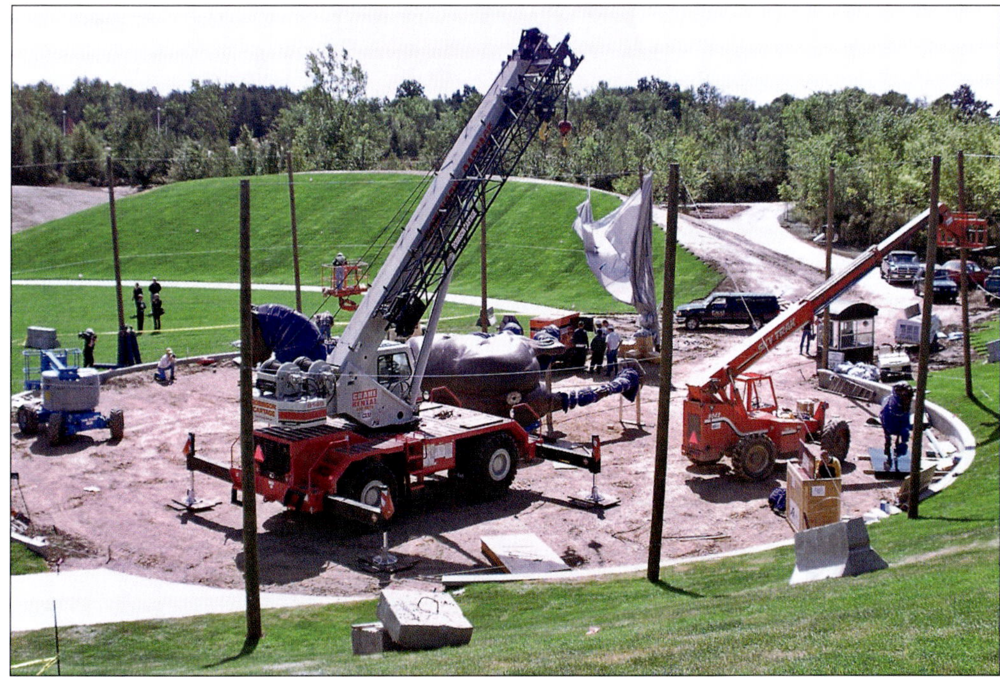

DeVos/Van Andel Piazza Photo by Dave Meinke

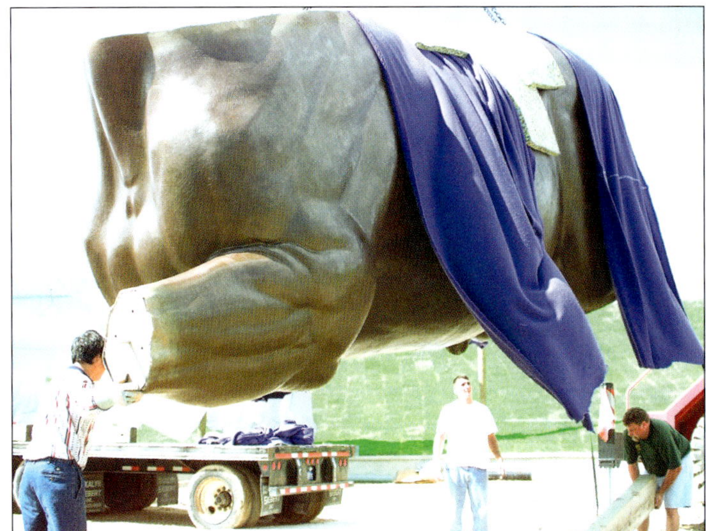
Unloading the torso Photo by Dave Meinke

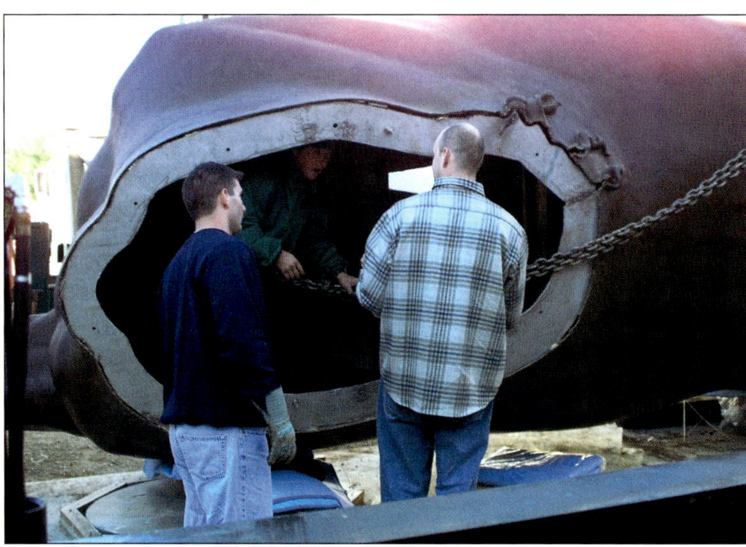
Preparing to make connections Photo by Dave Meinke

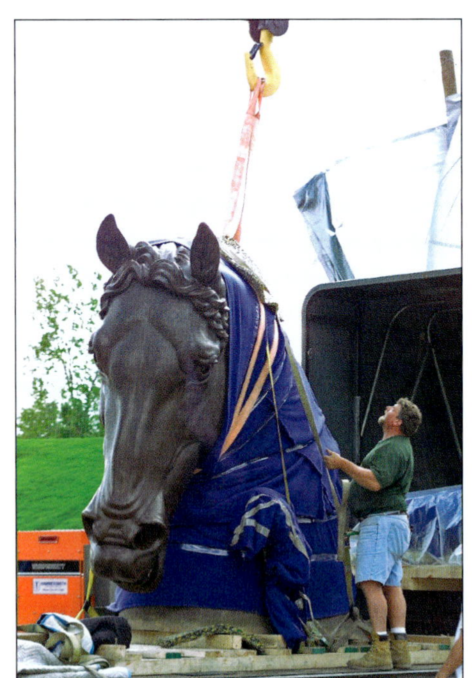
Unwrapping the head Photo by Dave Meinke

And when the sun came out for a few days, its surface baked into an uncooperative hardpan. Feuerstein came up with ways to shape the field into a plaza.

At the lower end was a natural swale that could serve as a creek, which could take the runoff from the field. On either side were areas that could be built into sweeping hills, allowing viewers to look at the horse from all sides, and even from above, if they were willing to climb a grassy slope. Finally, he designed a brick surface, later named the DeVos/Van Andel Piazza, near the center of the field. There the steed could be displayed to full advantage, with views from every side and all angles, high and low.

Once it had been trucked in from the foundry, *The American Horse* had to be mounted in preparation for its unveiling. While it was being assembled, there was an aura of secrecy and anticipation. High fences surrounded the work area, frustrating anyone who tried to sneak an advance peek. Construction workers, Meijer Gardens employees, select members of the media, and a few others were allowed past the guard stationed at the access gate. The gatekeeper maintained a clipboard with a list of authorized names.

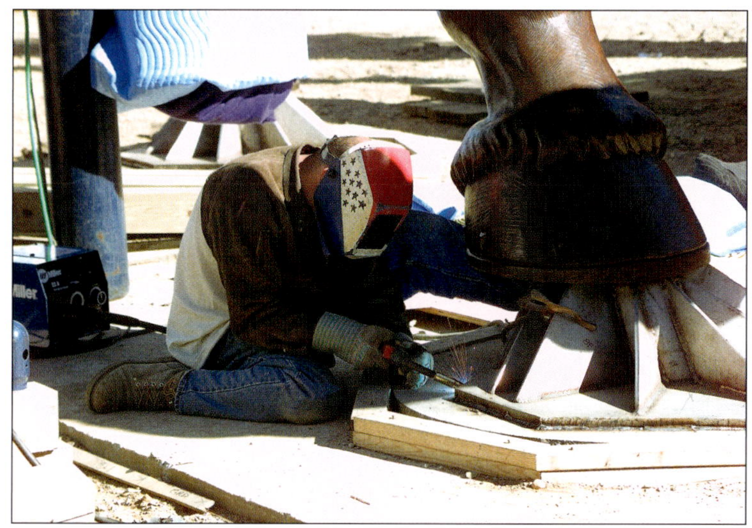

Anchoring plate Photo by Dave Meinke

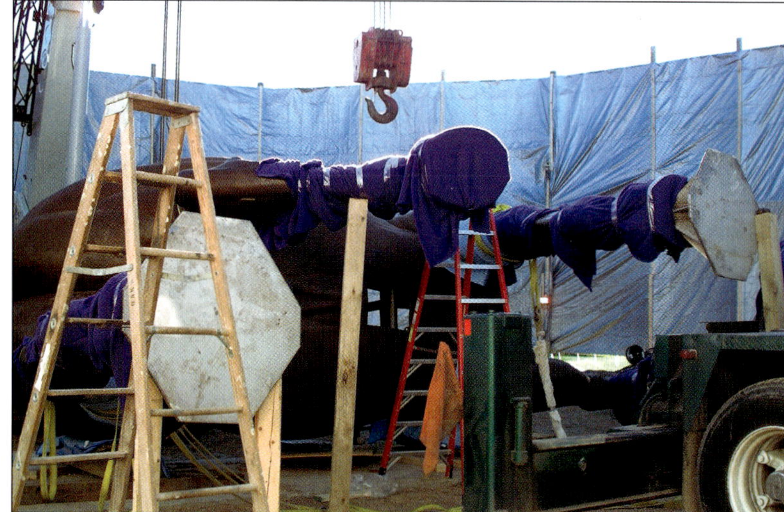

Assembling the torso Photo by Dave Meinke

The day after work began, Fred Meijer drove over to check the progress. He approached the gate and was stopped by the guard, who asked for his name and checked the list. Unfortunately, Fred's name wasn't there. The guard was under strict orders: he could allow access only to those whose names were listed. Fred was understanding.

"May I see the list?" he asked. He then wrote his name at the bottom — in big block letters. The guard let him in.

A horse standing on only two legs is a finicky creature. The pose may be artistically attractive, but when that horse weighs more than twenty thousand pounds, there's a chance that it may be dangerously unstable. Accordingly, structural engineers working with the foundry designed a stainless steel armature to fit inside the horse. Anchored by thick pipes running down the two legs that touch the ground, this armature was welded to heavy steel plates beneath the surface of the plaza. The support structure, completely hidden, adds four tons of weight, while ensuring that the horse can withstand a wind shear of as much as one hundred miles per hour.

Dave Meinke, a photographer for the Meijer Company, documented the last phase of construction in Grand Rapids. He recalls that as it was nearing completion, just before the last step — the reattachment of the head — "I found myself high in the air, standing in a cherry-picker, and thought it would be fun to toss my business card into the body of the horse as a personal token of my experience in the project. Later that day, I happened to be standing next to Fred and Lena when a friend of theirs walked over to them and said he'd seen someone toss a business card into the horse. I was embarrassed, but admitted I was the one who had done it. Fred thought that was a good idea. He wanted to do the same thing."

So Fred asked the construction workers to raise him and Lena up on a scissor-lift platform that would position them above the cavity where the head was to be placed. He took out a business card and a Purple Cow card — good for a free ice cream cone at any Meijer store (something Fred and Lena have given out thousands of times over

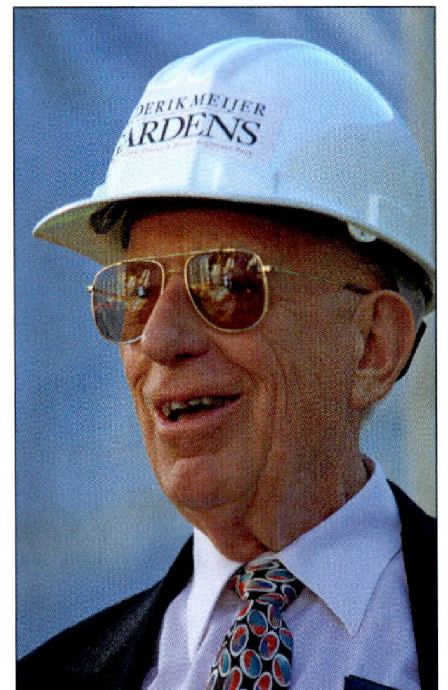

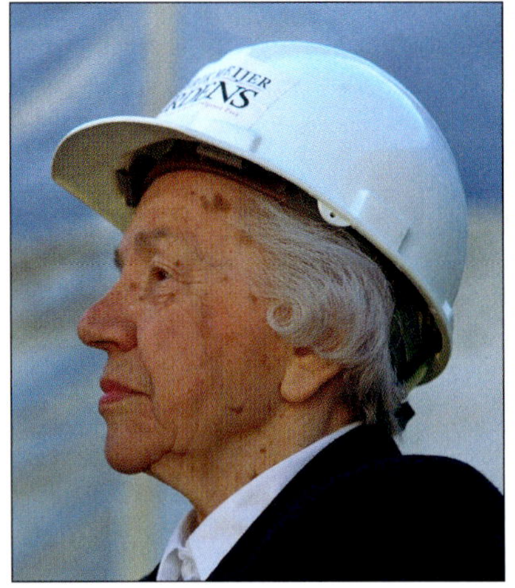

Fred Meijer and Lena Meijer

Photos by Dave Meinke

the years) — and dramatically dropped them into the horse while onlookers and news media cheered.

Now workers were ready to put the bronze behemoth together for the final time.

The worker standing inside the horse, bolting pieces together, finally escaped through a hatch in the belly. The seams were sealed and patinated by workers from the foundry. Then the machines departed and the piazza fell silent. The horse was draped in white muslin to await the official unveiling.

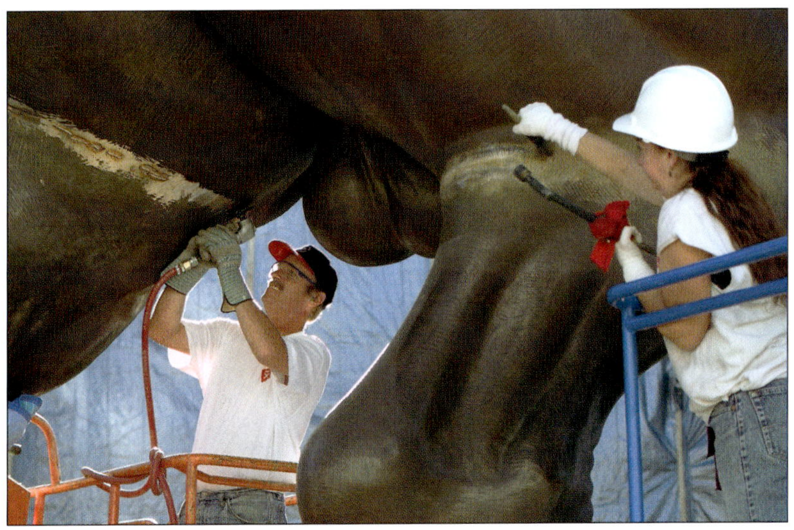

Hiding the seams Photo by Dave Meinke

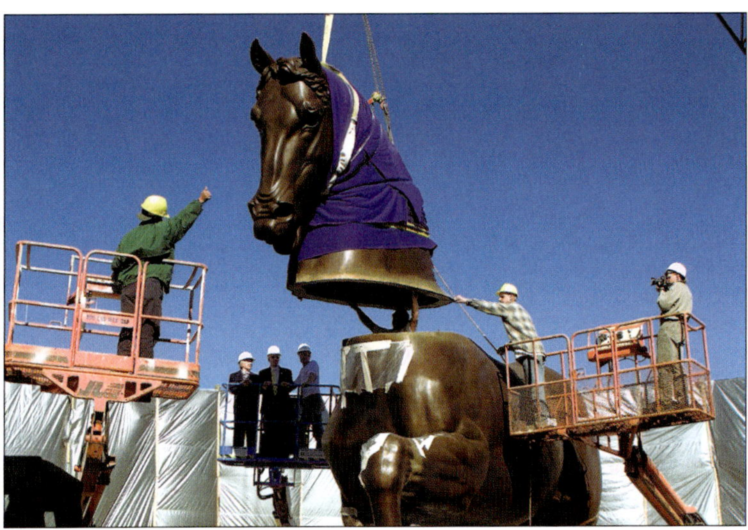

Nearing completion Photo by Dave Meinke

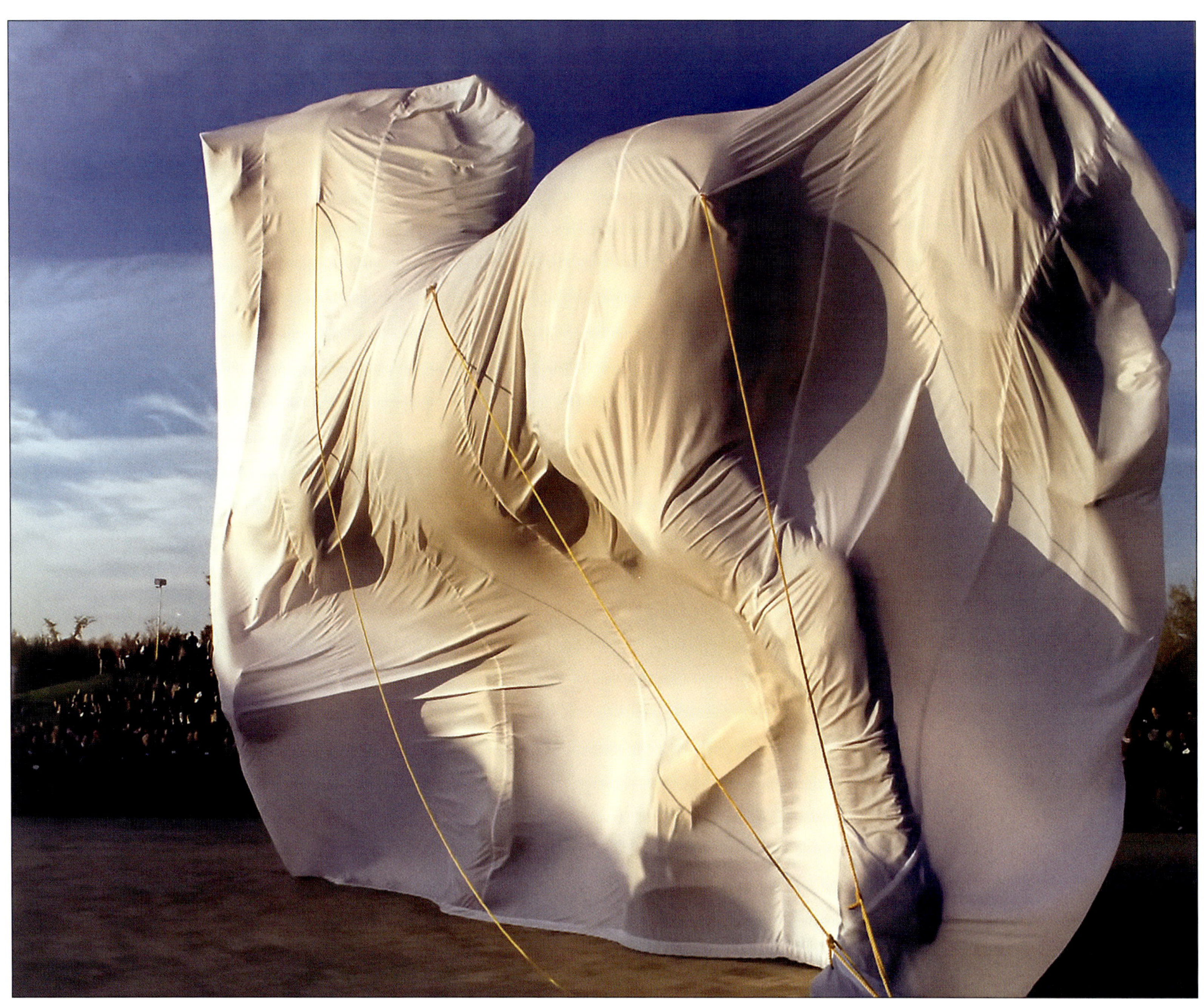

Sunset the day before unveiling

11. The Unveiling

The dedication of *The American Horse* took place on October 10, 1999. Ceremonies began in the morning, when sturdy Frisian draft horses pulled away the covering, revealing the massive charger to the West Michigan audience for the first time. The ceremonies continued throughout the day.

It was a grandly festive occasion, organized by a committee that included Sue Veeneman, Starr Meijer, Meg Miller Willett, and Pamella DeVos. Dan DeVos served as emcee; a military marching band, together with musicians from the Grand Rapids Symphony Orchestra, provided the music; and news organizations representing the major networks stationed their cameras around the periphery. Near the end of the evening an Olympic horse and rider performed dressage on the plaza, and the finale filled the sky with fireworks.

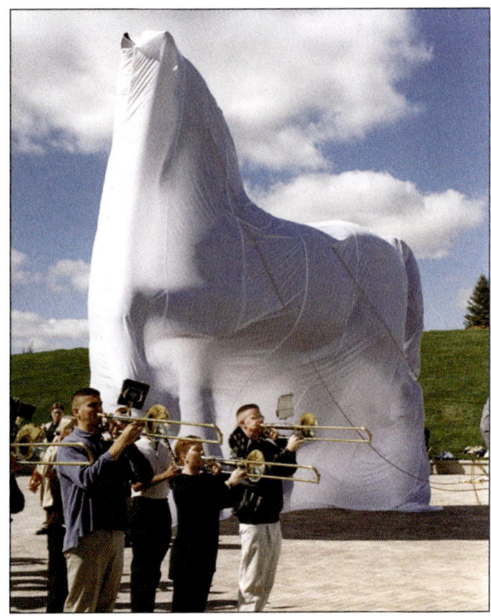
The ceremony begins

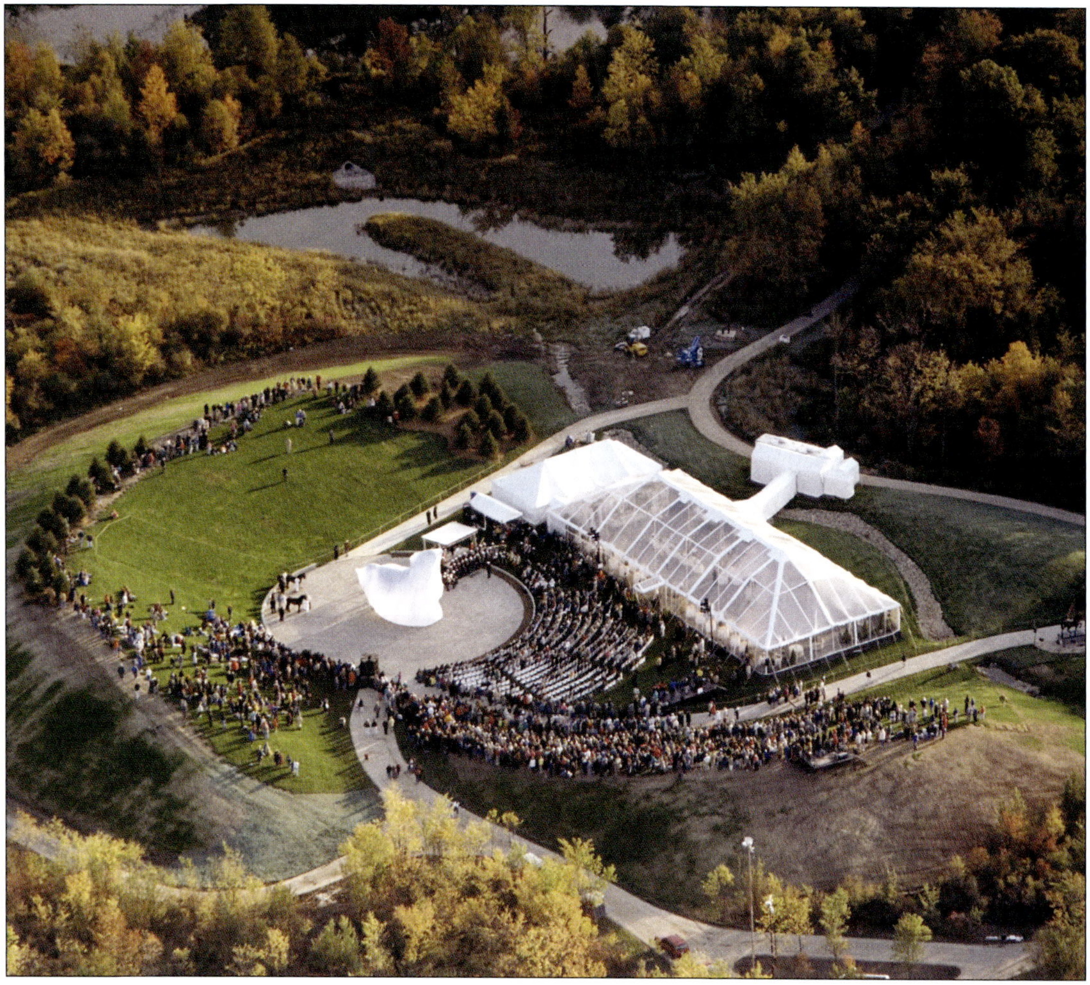

Aerial view before unveiling

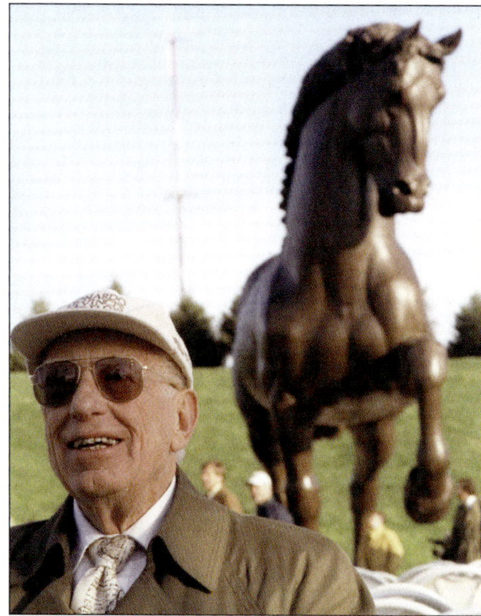

Fred Meijer

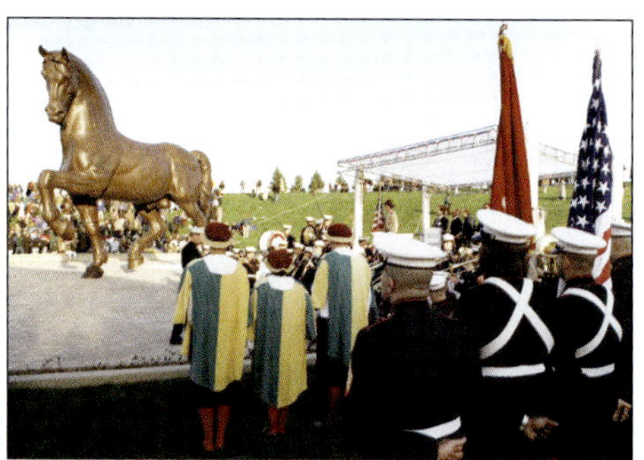

Fanfare

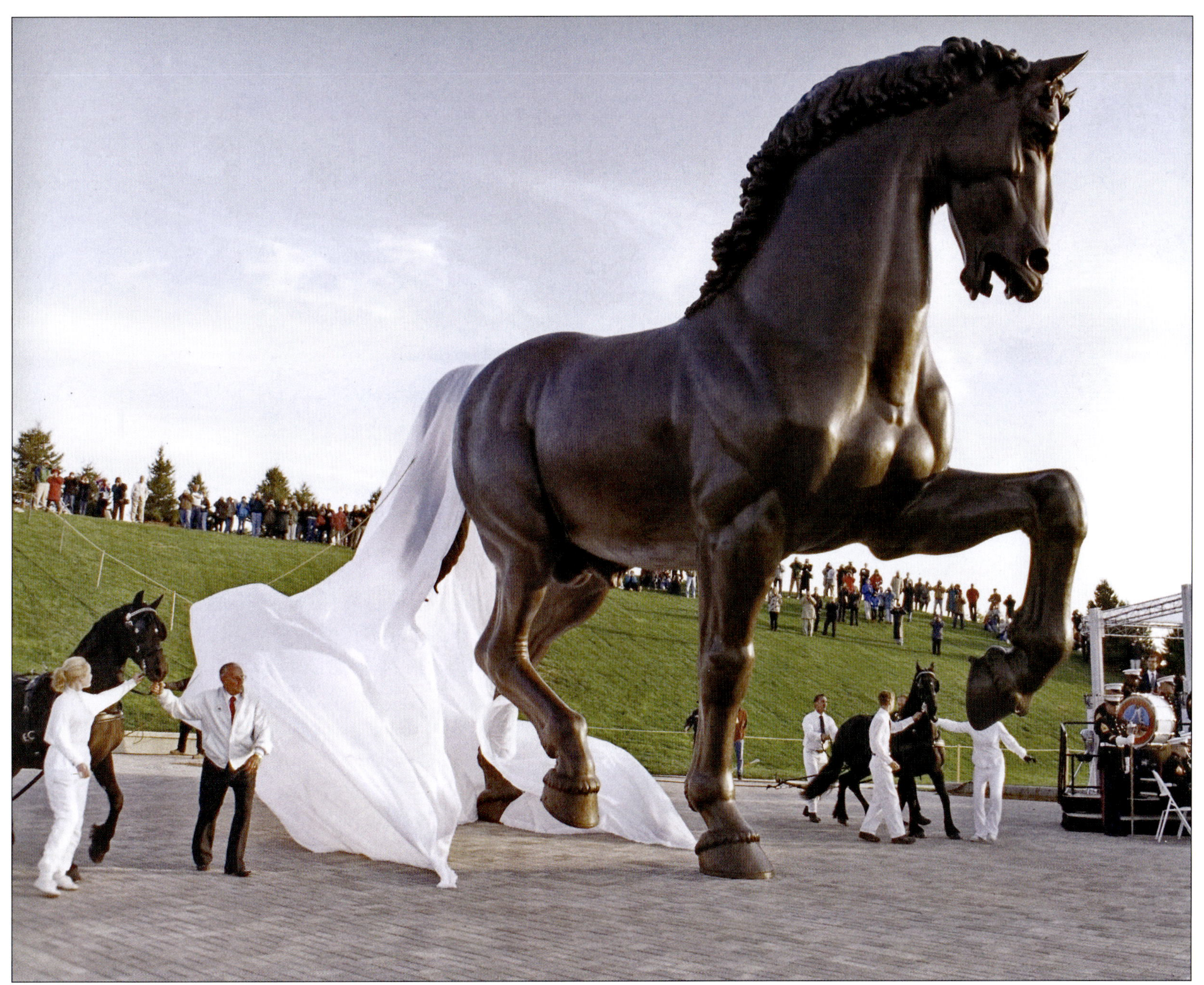

The unveiling

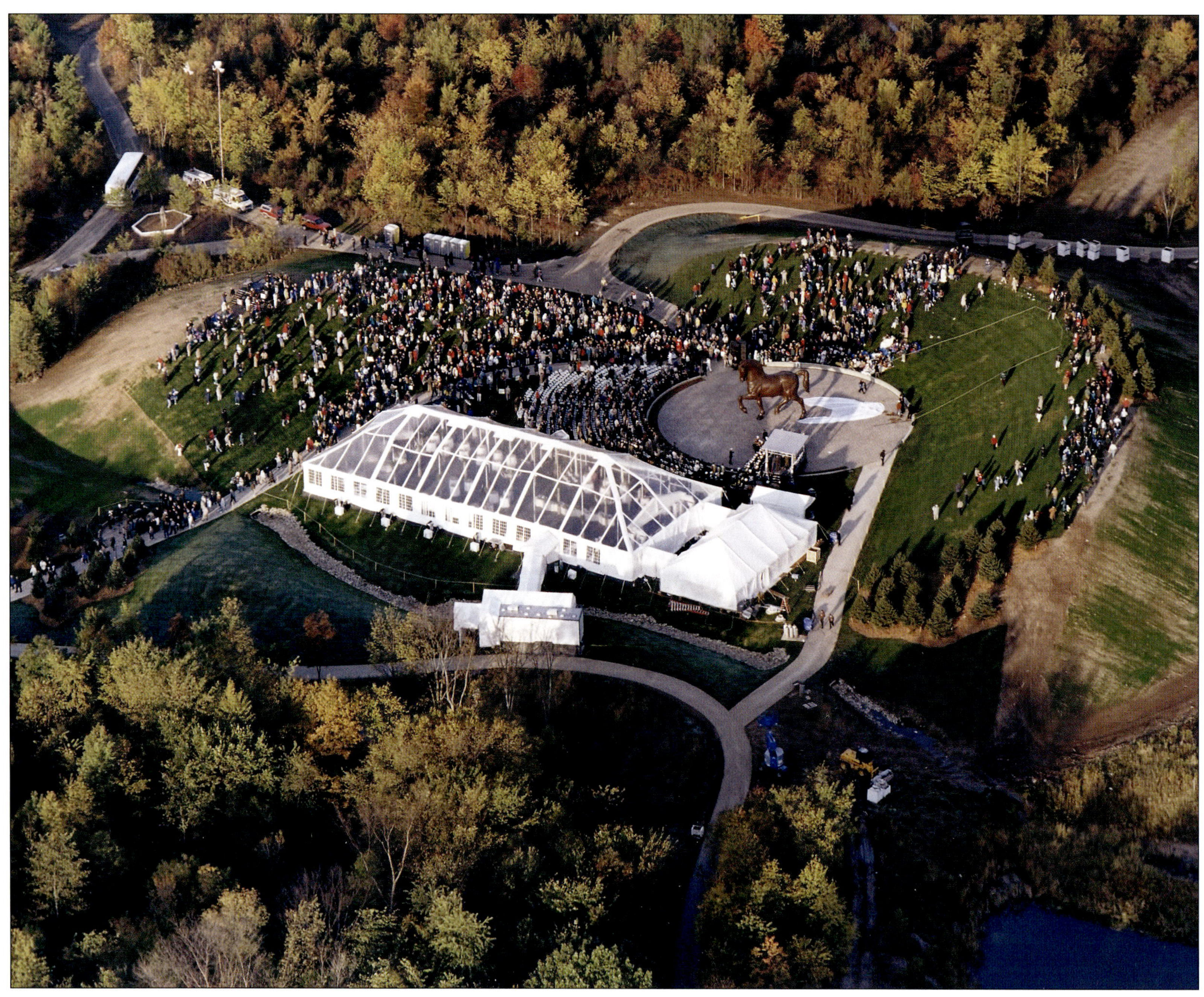
Aerial view after unveiling

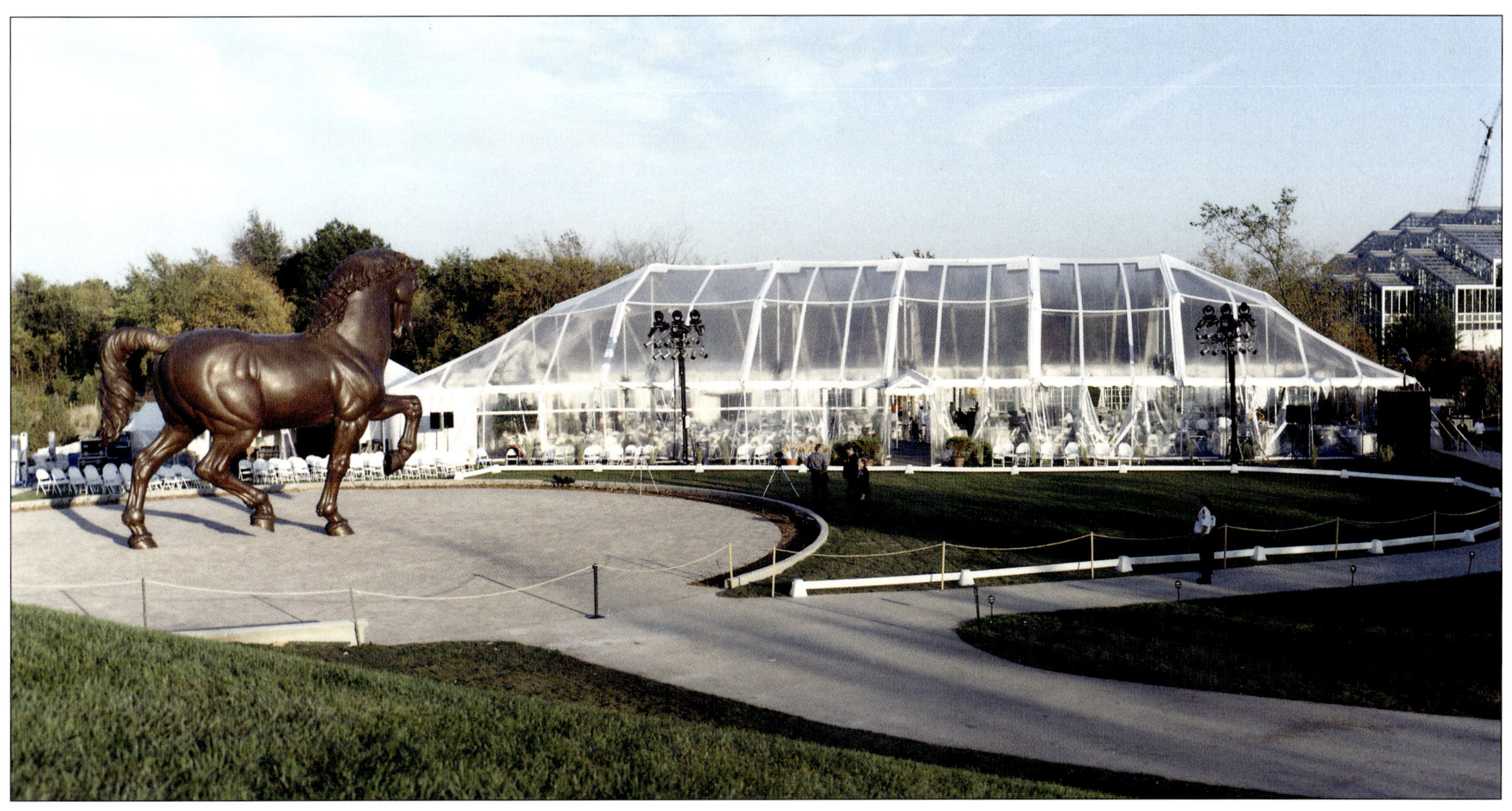

Preparing for the reception

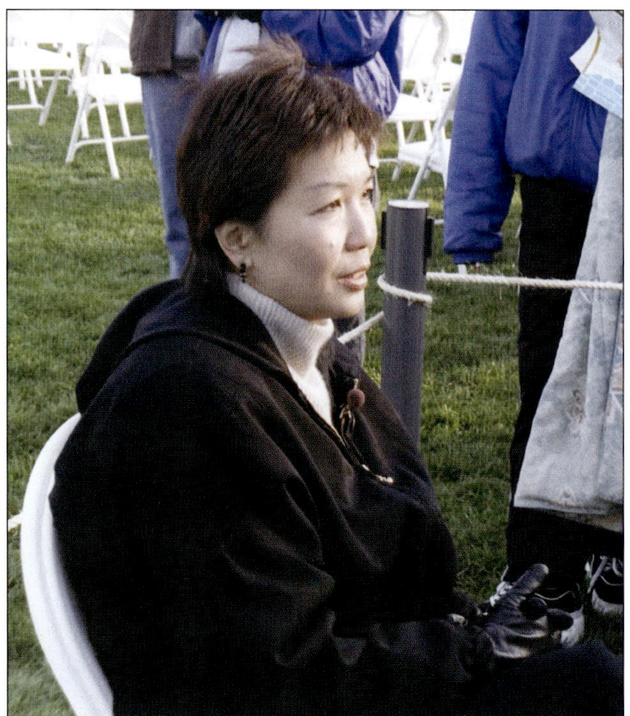

Nina Akamu

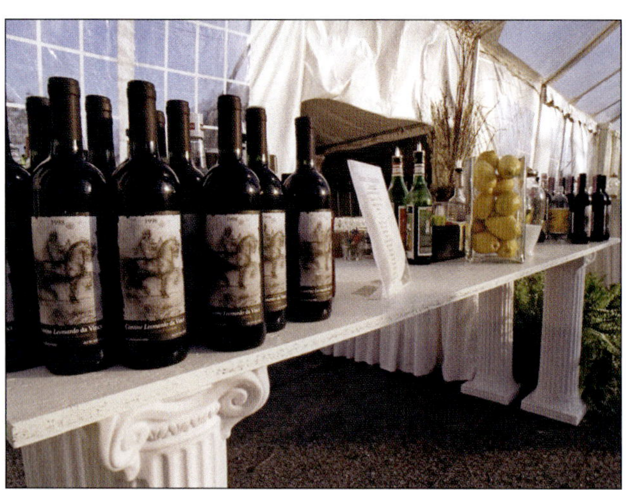

Renaissance chianti

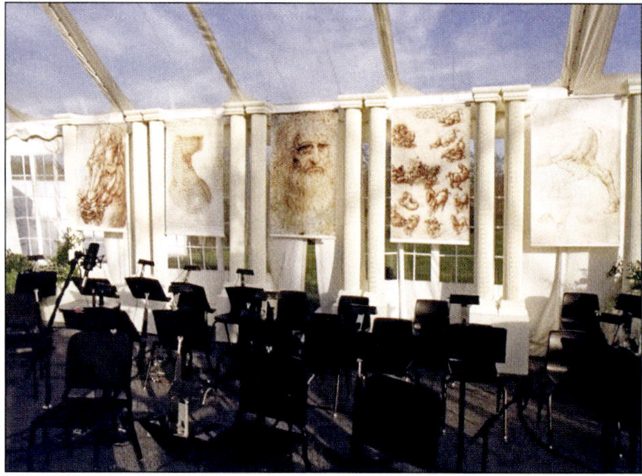

Orchestra pit

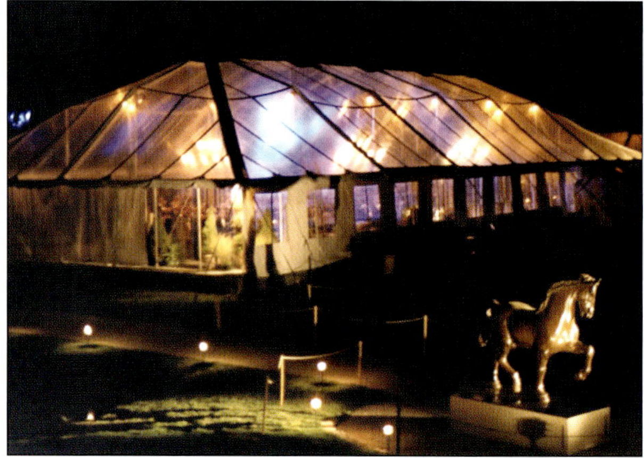

Reception in full swing

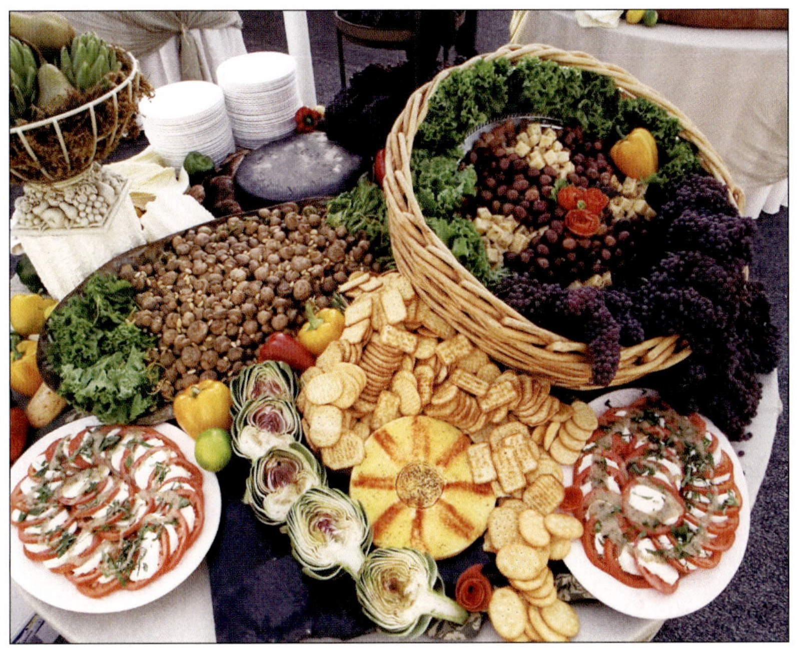

Fixings for banquet

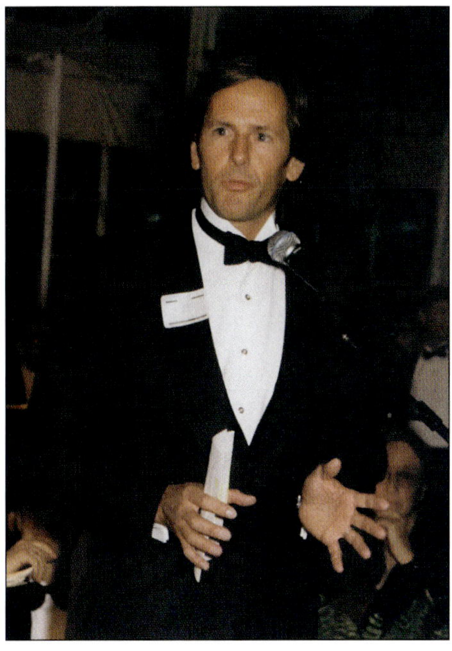

Emcee Dan DeVos

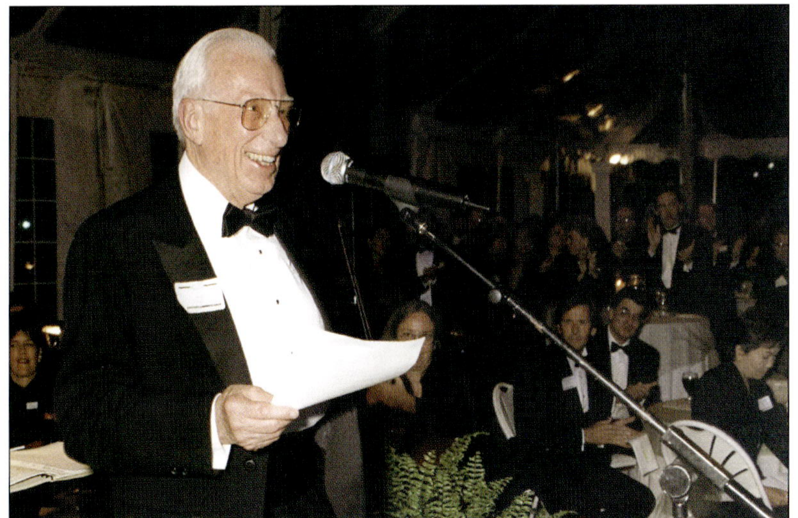

Fred reminisces

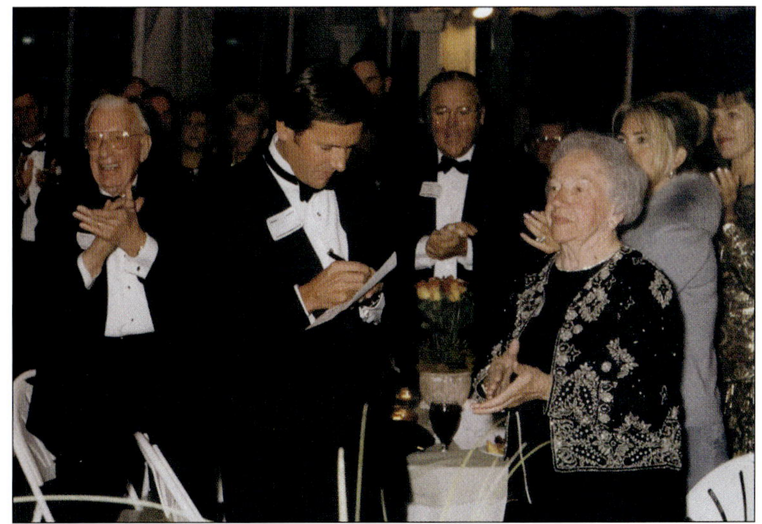

Fred Meijer, Dan DeVos, Peter Secchia, Lena Meijer, Pamella DeVos, Joan Secchia

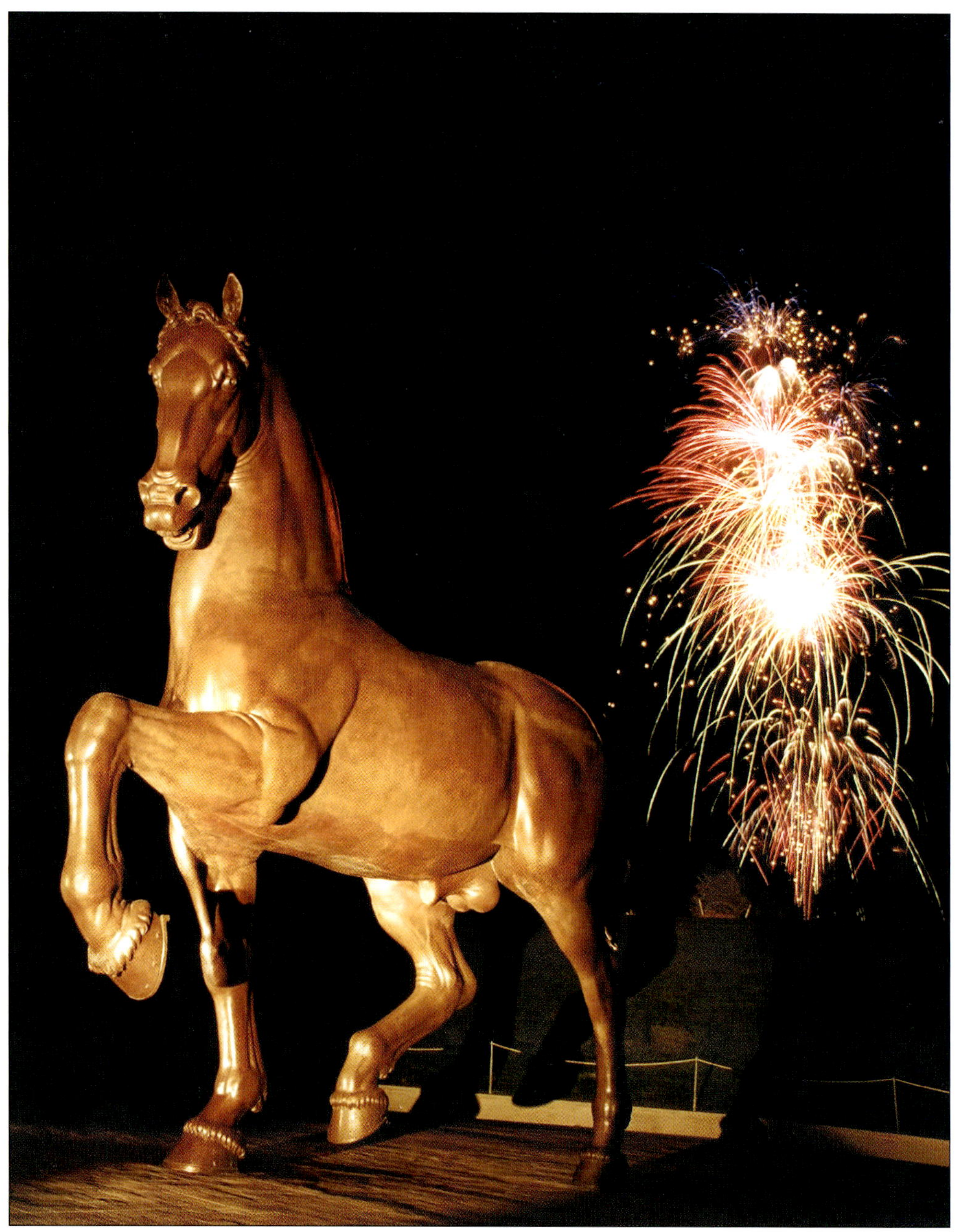

Fireworks

12. But Is It Art?

It should be clear by now that the equine tribute to Leonardo da Vinci cannot be discussed in quite the same way we discuss other works of art. We don't talk about the Statue of Liberty, the Lincoln Memorial, or Mount Rushmore as works of art in a primary sense, even though they embody a good deal of skill and demonstrate their artistry in compelling ways. But such monuments are important to the public imagination for reasons that go beyond what we generally think of as art. They are cultural monuments, best understood as expressions not of an individual artist's vision (the usual starting point for understanding contemporary works), but as one way a society celebrates values it holds dear.

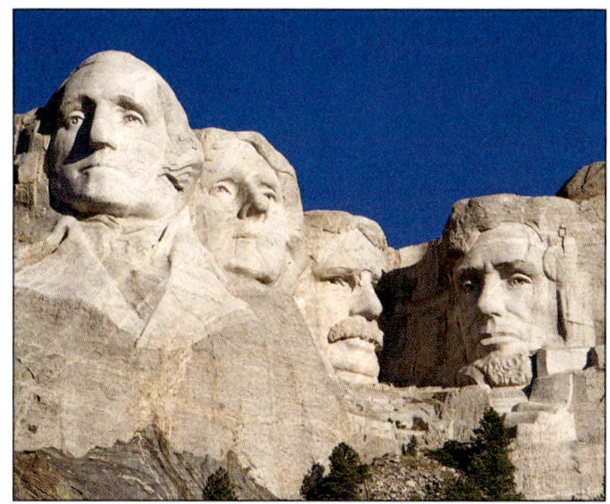

Wikimedia

The Presidents memorialized on Mount Rushmore, and the iconic appearance of their profiles against the western sky, are much more important in the public memory than is the artistic reputation of Gutzon Borglum, the sculptor who created it.

The same is true of the Lincoln Memorial. It is the great and tragic Civil War President sitting on a simple democratic version of a throne and staring out across the National Mall with a mixture of sadness and determination that gives that work its force. Sculptor Daniel Chester French (1850-1931) was noted in his lifetime for dozens of public sculptures, including the Concord Minute Man, the John Harvard Monument in Harvard Yard, the Samuel Francis du Pont Memorial in Wilmington, Delaware, and the Thomas Hopkins Gallaudet statue at Gallaudet University. French certainly had great artistic ability, but his work is not discussed in the same way as that of his

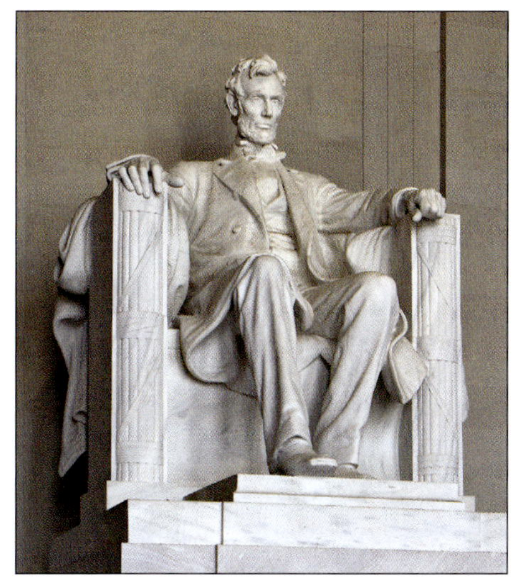

Wikimedia

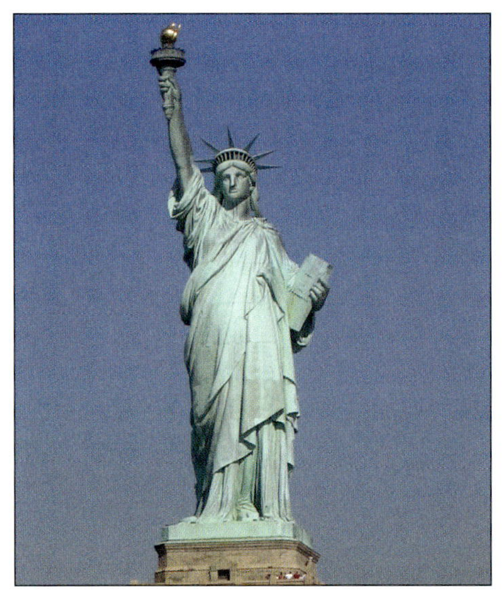

Wikimedia

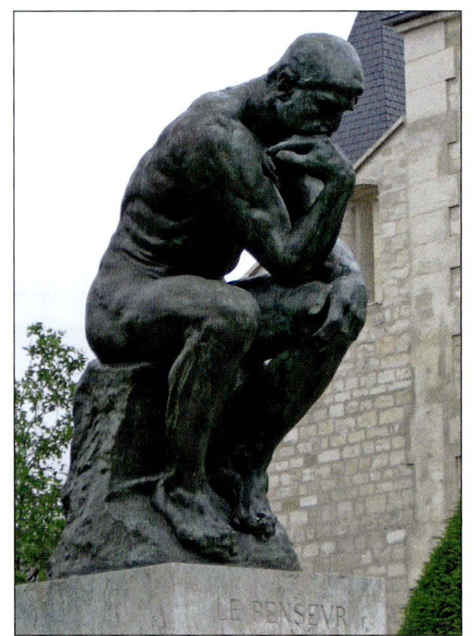

Auguste Rodin. *The Thinker*, Rodin Museum, Paris Photo by Larry ten Harmsel

near contemporary Auguste Rodin (1840-1917). Daniel Chester French created public art; Auguste Rodin changed the expressive vocabulary of sculpture in his era.

The Statue of Liberty (formally entitled *Liberty Enlightening the World*) provides another example of public or monumental art. Given by the people of France as a gift to America in 1886, it was sculpted by Frédéric-Auguste Bartholdi, with an internal structure designed by the engineer Maurice Koechlin, who also designed the Eiffel Tower. It is perhaps the best-known piece of sculpture in America, but it is never thought of or discussed in the same way as is, for example, *The Thinker,* another French work from the same era. It is not that one is necessarily "better" than the other; it's that they occupy different territories of the imagination.

These kinds of considerations are relevant to any discussion of Akamu's horse. It is both a twentieth-century monument and an homage to Renaissance forms and techniques. Renaissance scholar Carlo Pedretti calls Akamu's horse an example of *ekphrasis,* a Greek term meaning the expression of a work of art in a form different from the original.

Akamu was initially hired to complete a sculpture that was thought to be nearly finished. When it became clear that the Charles Dent horse was unfit for reproduction, she became the creator of a new model. But this creation was not simply her own. It was a unique amalgam of Leonardo's ideas, expressed in sketches and notes he had made; Renaissance notions of equestrian monuments, which Akamu had studied and visited during her twelve years of living and working in Italy; the demands of a committee (LDVHI) that continued to oversee the project and that also owned the rights to reproductions and commercial images; and the equally strong requirements of the principal donor, Fred Meijer, who with his advisors had insisted on final approval of the project.

In other words, like almost all public monuments, *The American Horse* is the product of a host of competing interests. It would be inappropriate to call it a piece of contemporary sculpture, since its creation was an attempt to capture the spirit of a 500-year-old idea for a nonexistent sculpture. And yet, despite the artistry and skill with which it has been executed, the horse is emphatically not a Renaissance work of art, certainly not a Leonardo sculpture. Since it is intended as an homage to Renaissance ideals symbolized by Leonardo, and embodied in a project he never completed, it seems best to look at the horse as the expression of an ideal, as all monuments attempt to be. It is not Leonardo's "grand charger"; that doesn't exist. But it is as close as anyone is likely to come to the completion of one of Leonardo's dreams, and it came to completion in the hands of the sculptor Nina Akamu.

"Because of his name recognition, it's a pretty easy sell to connect it to Leonardo," laments Joe Becherer. "I often feel that Nina's work has been given short shrift. It's been a battle ever since, to show the power and vigor of her work, and to give her proper credit."

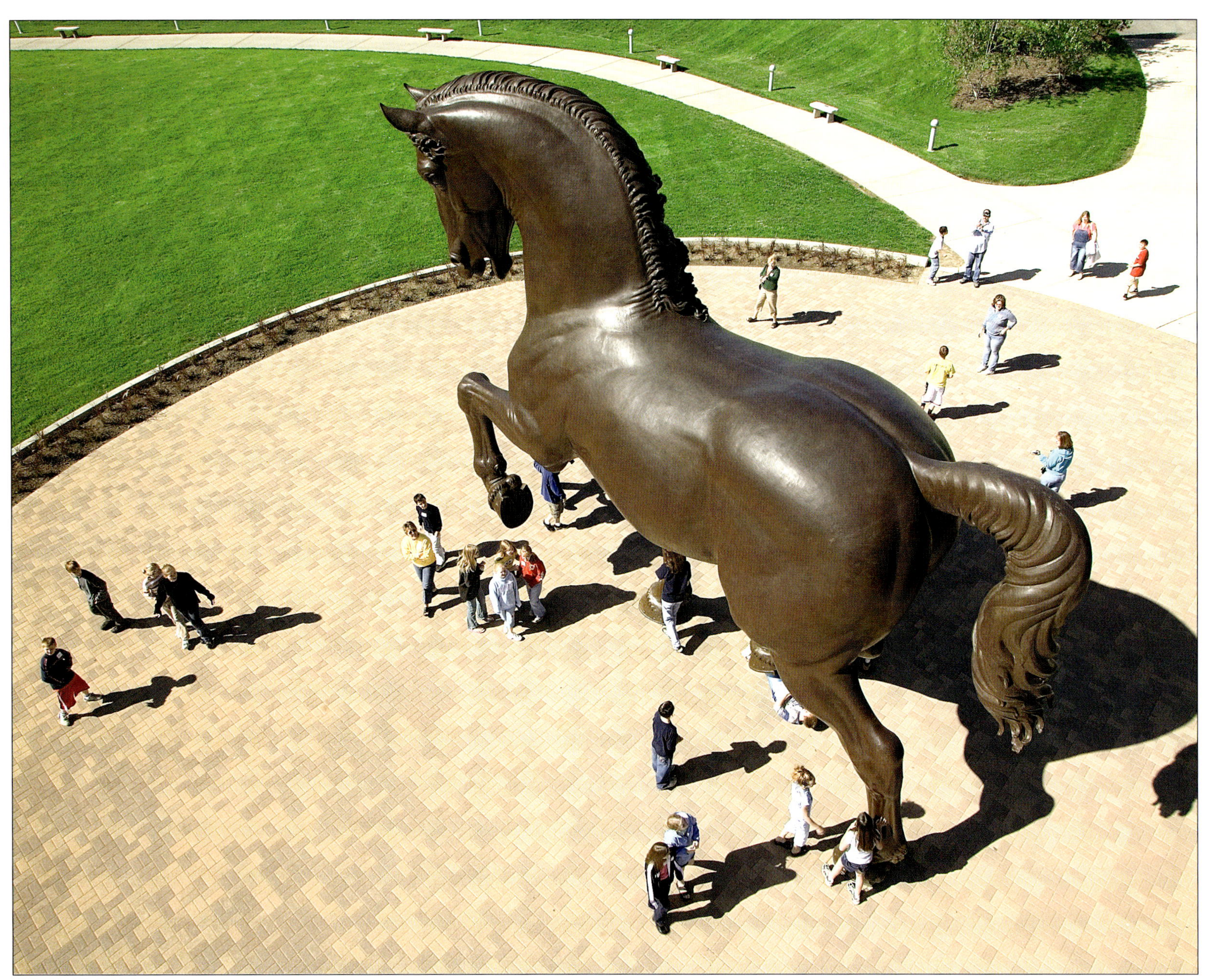

Aerial view

13. Riding into the Future

The American Horse was unveiled near the end of a second phase of the construction of Meijer Gardens. A beautiful rounded room with a wall of windows, formerly the café, became the Arthur and Elizabeth Snell Sculpture Center, a space dedicated to educating visitors about sculpture. Up to that point, the idea of art education at Meijer Gardens was underdeveloped. In fact, some of the early artistic materials used the farm animals and were essentially butcher's diagrams. With the transformation of the former café, there was now a chance to tell the story of the development of the horse — and the development of sculpture generally. To that end, Akamu's eight-foot horse, *Homage to Leonardo,* was placed in the Snell Center. There it stood for the next decade. It was always a bit too big for the room that housed it, so the horse often seemed poised for a trot into the open space that beckoned just outside the curving wall of windows.

The center was designed to give viewers of all ages a basis for understanding sculpture and to suggest several approaches for looking at particular works in Meijer Gardens' expanding collection. Over those next ten years, some four million visitors came to Meijer Gardens, about three hundred thousand of them schoolchildren.

Homage to Leonardo was surrounded by an ever-changing array of displays explaining its history, showing how it was created, discussing the methods of casting used by the foundry, and putting this work into the larger context of the world of sculpture by focusing on a host of other artists featured in the collection: Richard

Many cultures have prized bronze for its durability and lustrous surface. Because bronze casts are made from molds of wax or clay models, an artist can achieve great detail.

There are two main methods for bronze casting—sand casting, often used for flat surfaces, and lost wax casting, used for greater detail. Both the 8-foot *Homage to Leonardo* and the 24-foot *American Horse*, like many other sculptures, were created using a combination of these two methods. The following steps outline the sand casting method:

- Creation of scale model in clay
- Molds made from model
- Molds removed from model in sections
- Sections filled with plaster (more durable than clay) to create a plaster mold
- Plaster mold encased in a mixture of sand and cement in a box
- Mixture hardened and plaster molds removed from box
- Box closed and molten bronze poured into impression left by plaster mold
- Bronze form removed from box after cooling
- Bronze pieces welded together
- Bronze cleaned and finished

Hunt, Barbara Hepworth, Mark di Suvero, Auguste Rodin, Aristide Maillol, Deborah Butterfield, Henry Moore, and many others.

For a decade this display allowed docents and educators to help visitors understand sculpture more fully. Visitors to the Snell Center were encouraged to begin an educational process similar to what had occurred with Fred and Lena Meijer. As it turned out, the couple had begun a long educational odyssey when they decided to get involved with the creation of the monumental horse, a journey that led them into encounters with an astonishing array of artists and sculptures.

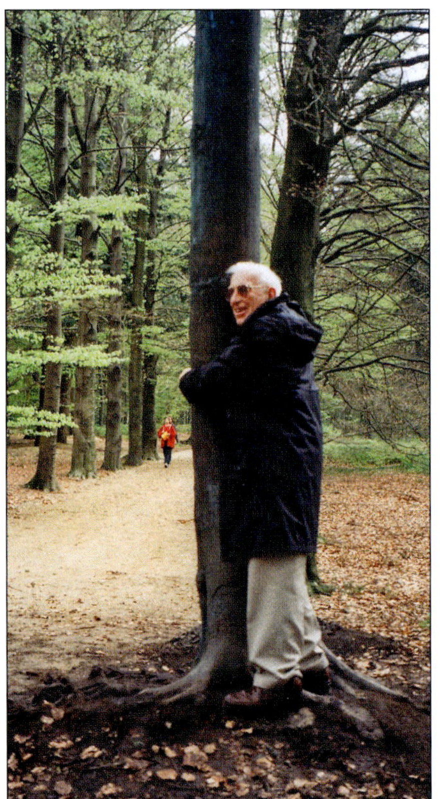

Fred Meijer at Kröller-Müller Museum

Photo by Larry ten Harmsel

As part of that process, Fred and Lena Meijer made several visits to the Kröller-Müller Museum in Otterlo, the Netherlands. One of Europe's premier outdoor sculpture collections, the Kröller-Müller was an early inspiration for Frederik Meijer Gardens & Sculpture Park. During one of those trips, while learning what he could about the expense involved in the acquisition, display, and maintenance of sculpture, Fred demonstrated, with typical forthrightness, his visceral approach to art. He was struck by a tall slender tower made of a delicate lacing of cables and stainless steel tubes by the American Kenneth Snelson. So he went over to it and lay on his back beneath it. Asked why he was doing that, he replied, "I want to see if it moves in the wind." He lay there a while, looking up into the sky. Asked what he had concluded, he said, "Can't tell — the clouds are moving, too."

A few minutes later, still filled with an antic spirit, he saw a bronze beech tree by Italian sculptor Giuseppe Penone. It was displayed on a path in the woods, occupying a spot where one tree in a row of beeches had died. Meijer went over to hug it. "The world," he said, "can always use another tree-hugger."

Sculpture Advisory Committee member Bill Padnos, former managing director of the Oxbow Art School in Saugatuck, explains how he sees the outcome of this process of education:

> *I was never overwhelmed with the whole concept of the horse, but I was willing to go along with it because of Fred's commitment. To this day, however, I think Fred understood something I didn't get at the time: he sensed what a crowd-pleaser it would be. It brings people in, and engages people who might not otherwise consider sculpture in a serious way.*
>
> *Serious sculpture-lovers don't spend much time discussing the horse — they want to talk about the rest of the collection. But our situation at Meijer Gardens is in some ways unique in the art world. We have myriad entry points for people who would not otherwise come to a sculpture museum: the farm garden, the horse, the concerts, the children's garden, and, of course, the horticultural displays. That's not something a traditional museum is able to do.*
>
> *We bring in many more people who do not come primarily for art than, for example, the Walker does in Minneapolis. That*

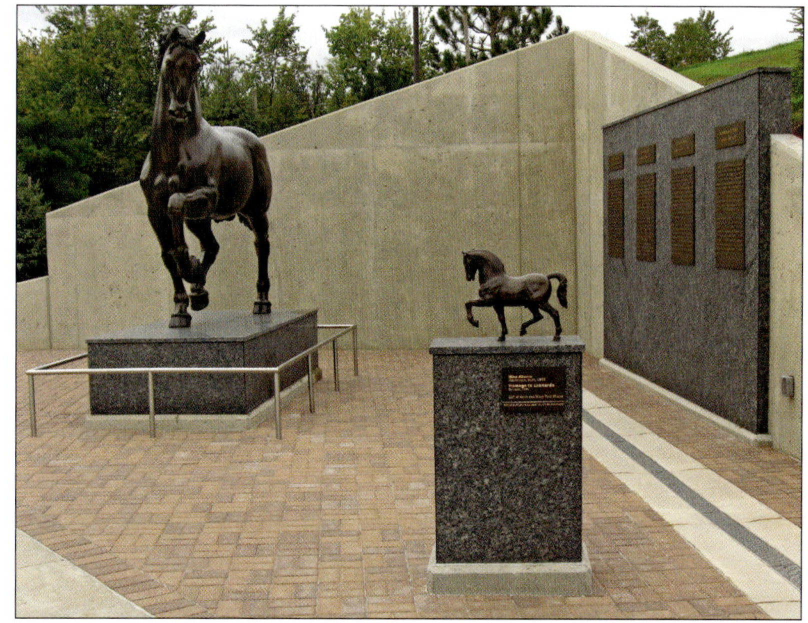

Educational plaza Photo by Larry ten Harmsel

gives us opportunities for expanding the audience that other institutions do not have, to lead people to a further understanding and appreciation of art. You've got to get them in the door first, and many people who come here would not come through the door of a traditional art museum.

Padnos concludes, "We bring in a lot more people who do not start out with an interest in fine art, and we provide an easy access that other institutions may not have."

On September 22, 2009, Meijer Gardens celebrated the ten-year anniversary of the unveiling of *The American Horse.* An outdoor educational space was created, designed by Assistant Curator Caleb Brennan, to display four bronze plaques outlining a brief history of the horse; a fifteen-inch casting intended especially for visitors with visual impairments; a description of the project in Braille; and a marble pediment holding *Homage to Leonardo,* the master model from which both the twenty-four-foot giant and the fifteen-inch miniature were made. Finally, the eight-foot horse was released from its indoor stable and put back where it belonged, in the company of its enormous offspring.

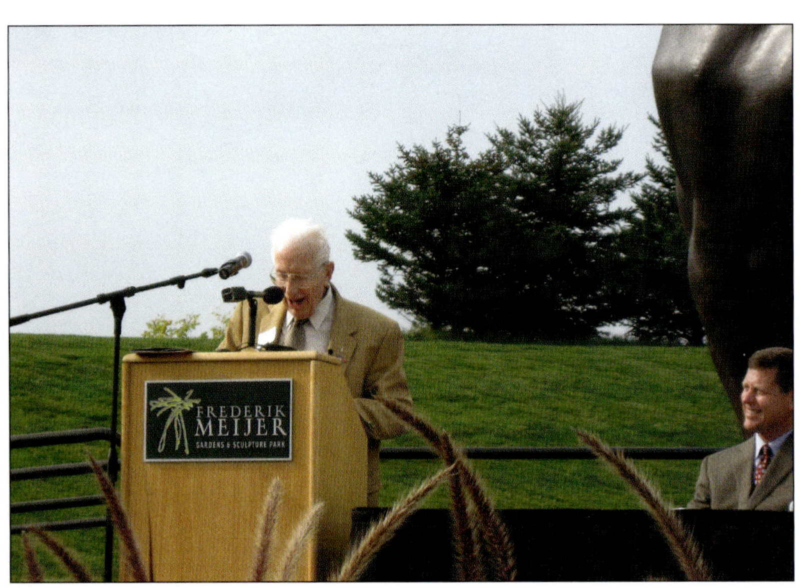

Fred Meijer and David Hooker at ten-year celebration

When Fred Meijer stood at the lectern to speak, he joked that ten years earlier, when he was only eighty, he'd had an easier time of it. Then he reminisced about the excitement of the project, thanked many of the people who had been involved, and relished the growing reputation of the institution that bore his name.

Reminiscing about the fifteen years that have passed since the opening of Frederik Meijer Gardens & Sculpture Park, he wondered what kind of exciting changes the coming years would bring to what he considers his most important legacy. "Fifteen years from now," he concluded, with a wry smile, "I'll be a hundred and five years old. I can only hope that I'll still be able to enjoy this marvelous institution."

For millions of visitors to Frederik Meijer Gardens & Sculpture Park, *The American Horse* has come to symbolize a journey of the imagination. We have no idea where this horse ride will take us, but it's sure to be exciting.

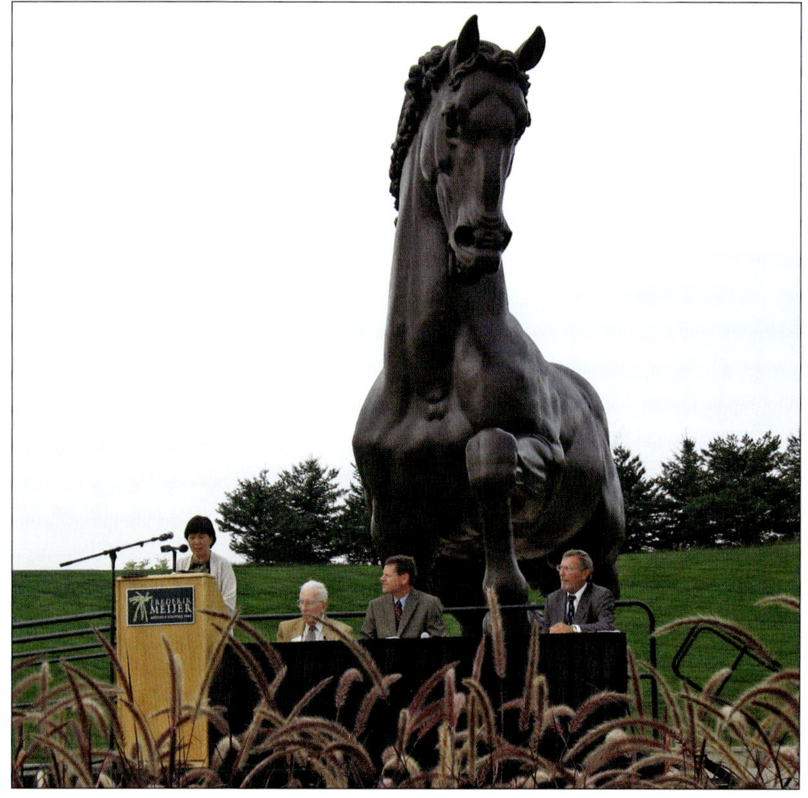

Nina Akamu, Fred Meijer, David Hooker, Larry ten Harmsel

The Story Continues

The photos on the following pages show a sample of the sculpture acquired by Frederik Meijer Gardens & Sculpture Park within two years of the completion and installation of *The American Horse.* These works helped form the core of the Sculpture Park, dedicated in 2002. They are part of an increasingly significant collection that continues to grow in complexity, recognition, and critical acclaim.

In 2005, *The Wall Street Journal* wrote, "There's nothing quite like Frederik Meijer Gardens & Sculpture Park this side of the Kröller-Müller Museum in The Netherlands."

In 2009, Patricia Schultz, author of *1,000 Places to See Before You Die,* named Frederik Meijer Gardens & Sculpture Park one of the top thirty must-see museums in the world, including institutions such as the Louvre, the Uffizi, the Guggenheim Bilbao, MoMA, and the Getty Center in Los Angeles. Number twelve on her list was the Van Gogh Museum in Amsterdam. Number thirteen was Frederik Meijer Gardens & Sculpture Park.

In 2010, a worldwide survey of attendance at cultural institutions placed Frederik Meijer Gardens & Sculpture Park in the top one hundred, with 504,488 visitors. Such recognition is important because it continues to establish this organization as an epicenter for culture in the Midwest.

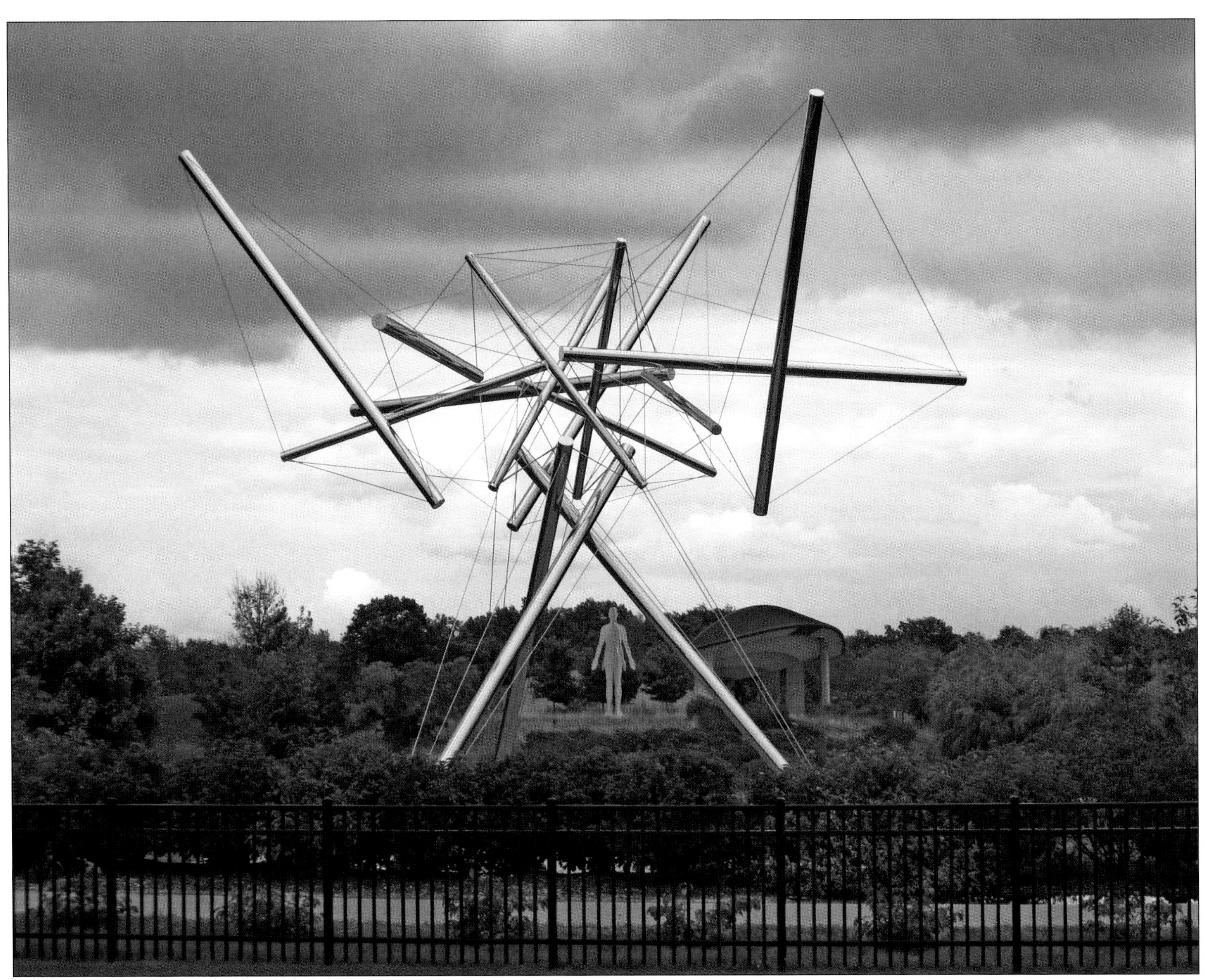

Kenneth Snelson. ***B-Tree II*****, 2005.** Photo by Larry ten Harmsel

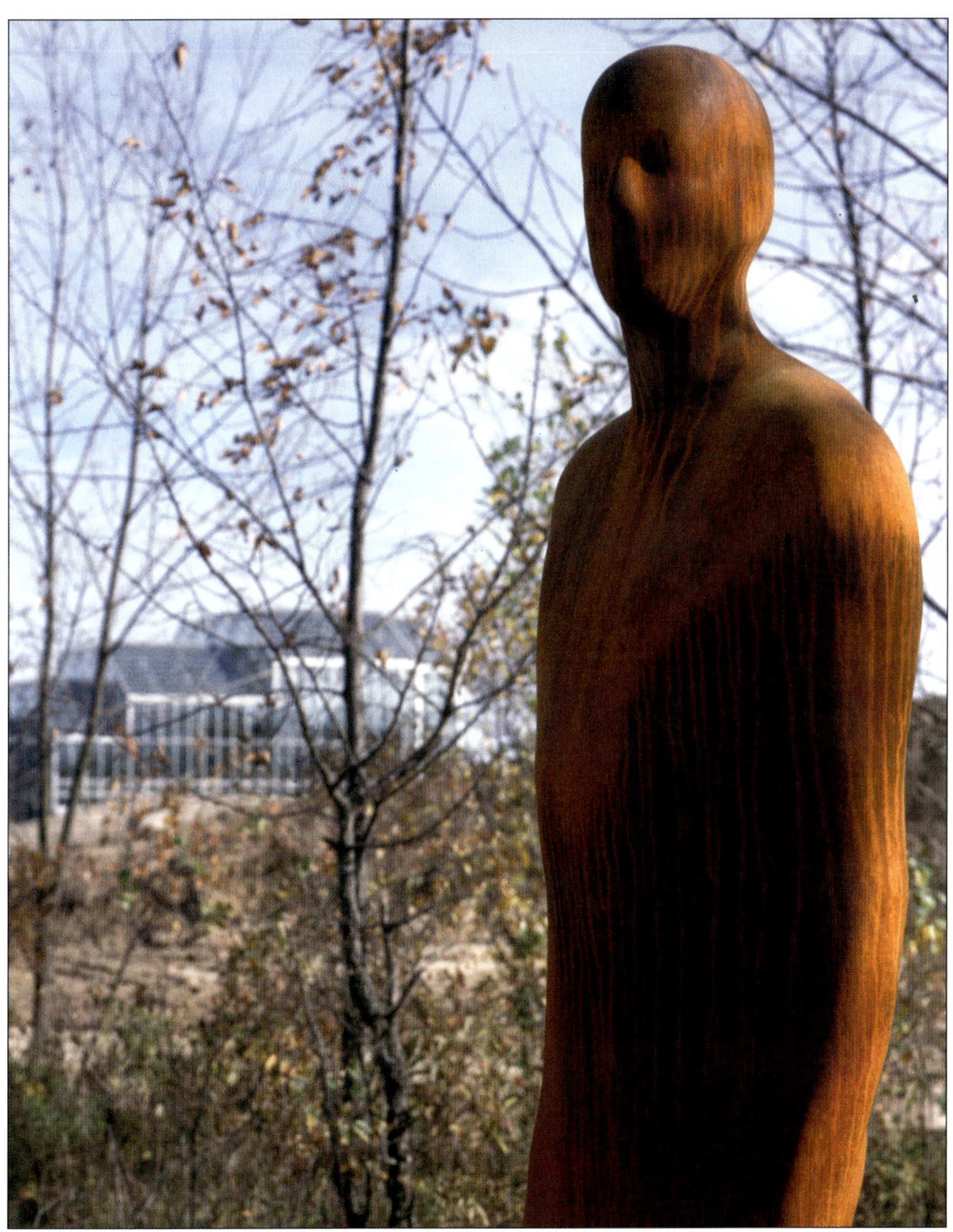

Antony Gormley. *One and Other,* 2000. Photo by William J. Hebert

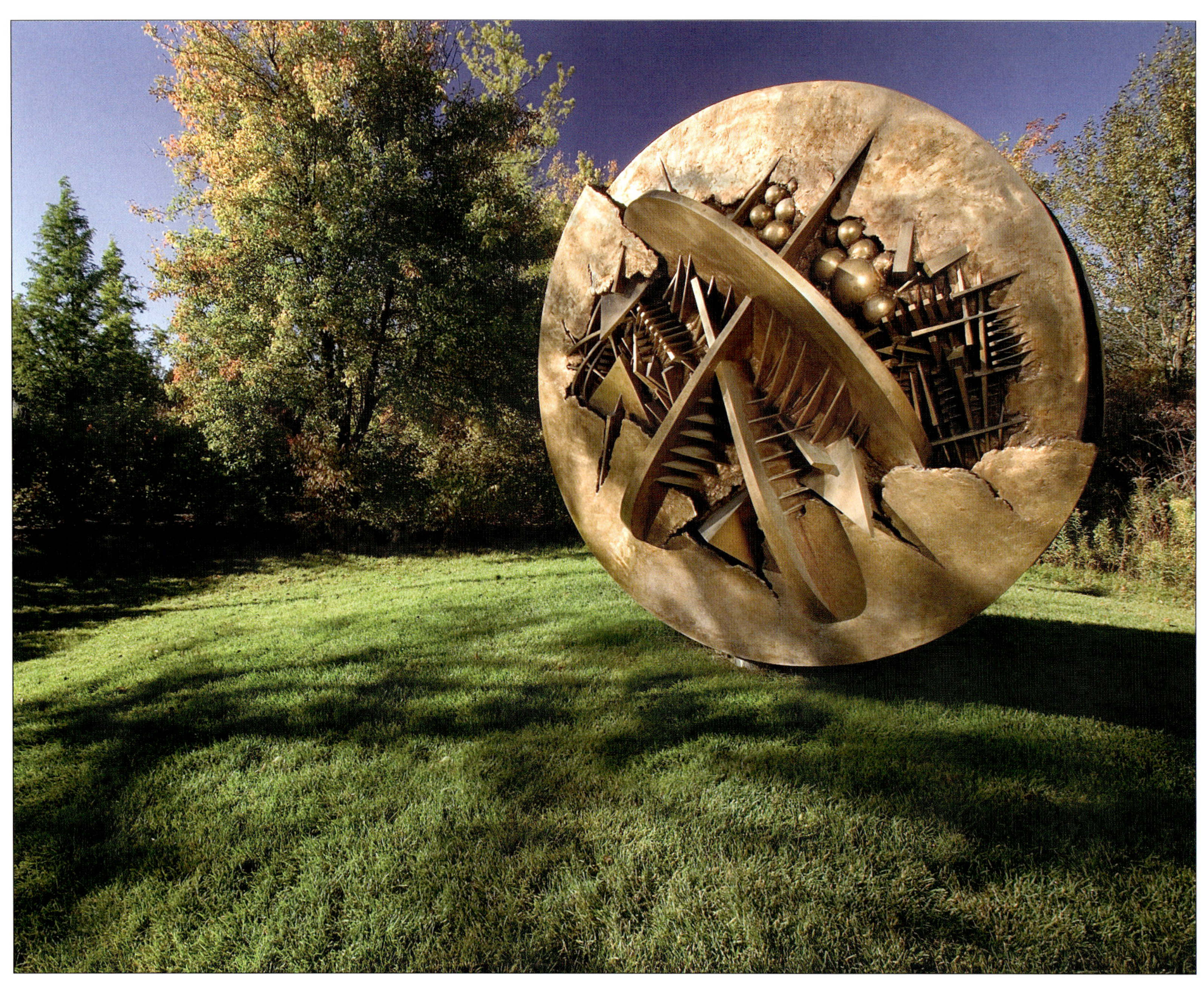

Arnaldo Pomodoro. *Disk in the Form of a Desert Rose*, 1993–1994. Photo by William J. Hebert

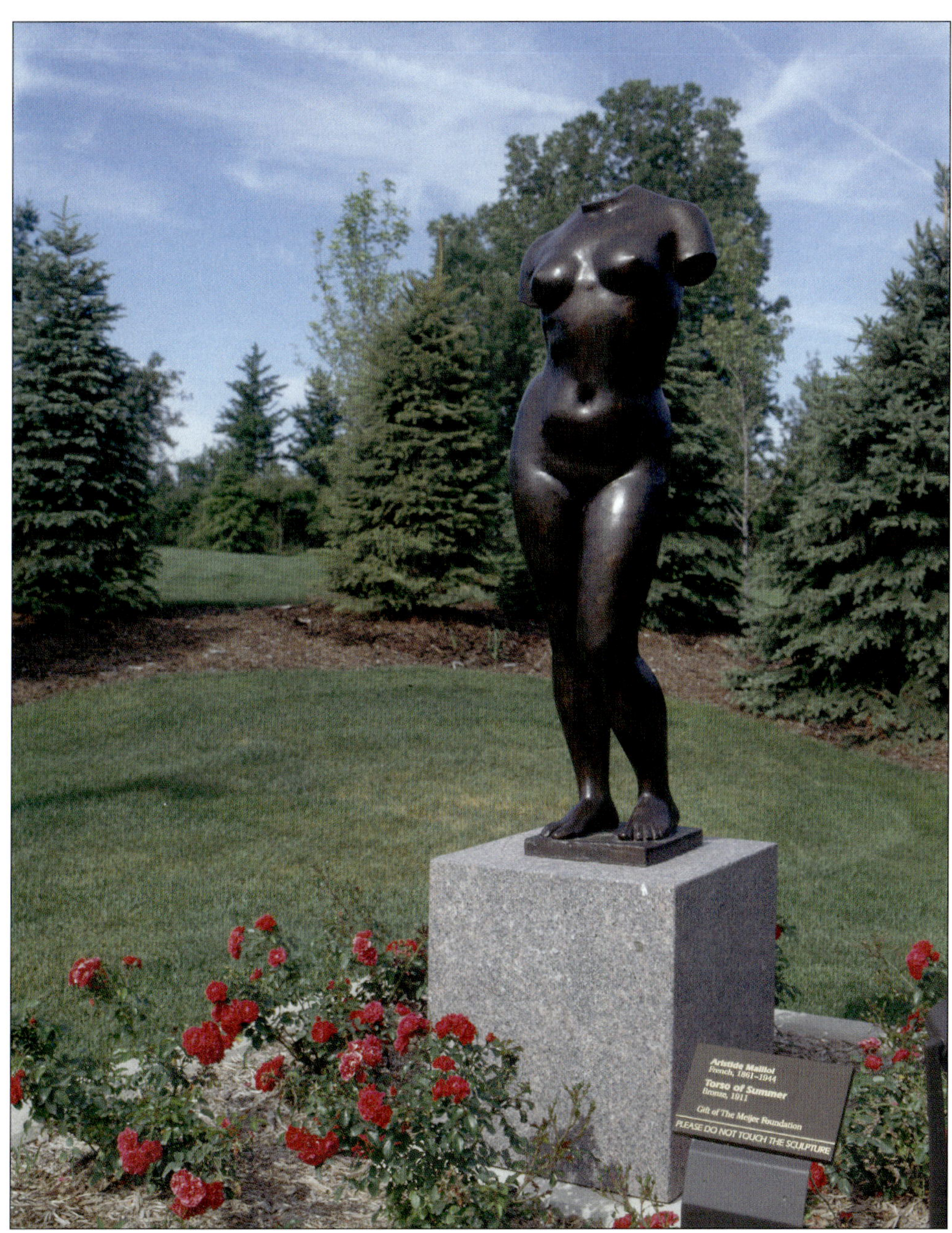

Aristide Maillol. *Torso of Summer,* 1911. Photo by Chuck Heiney

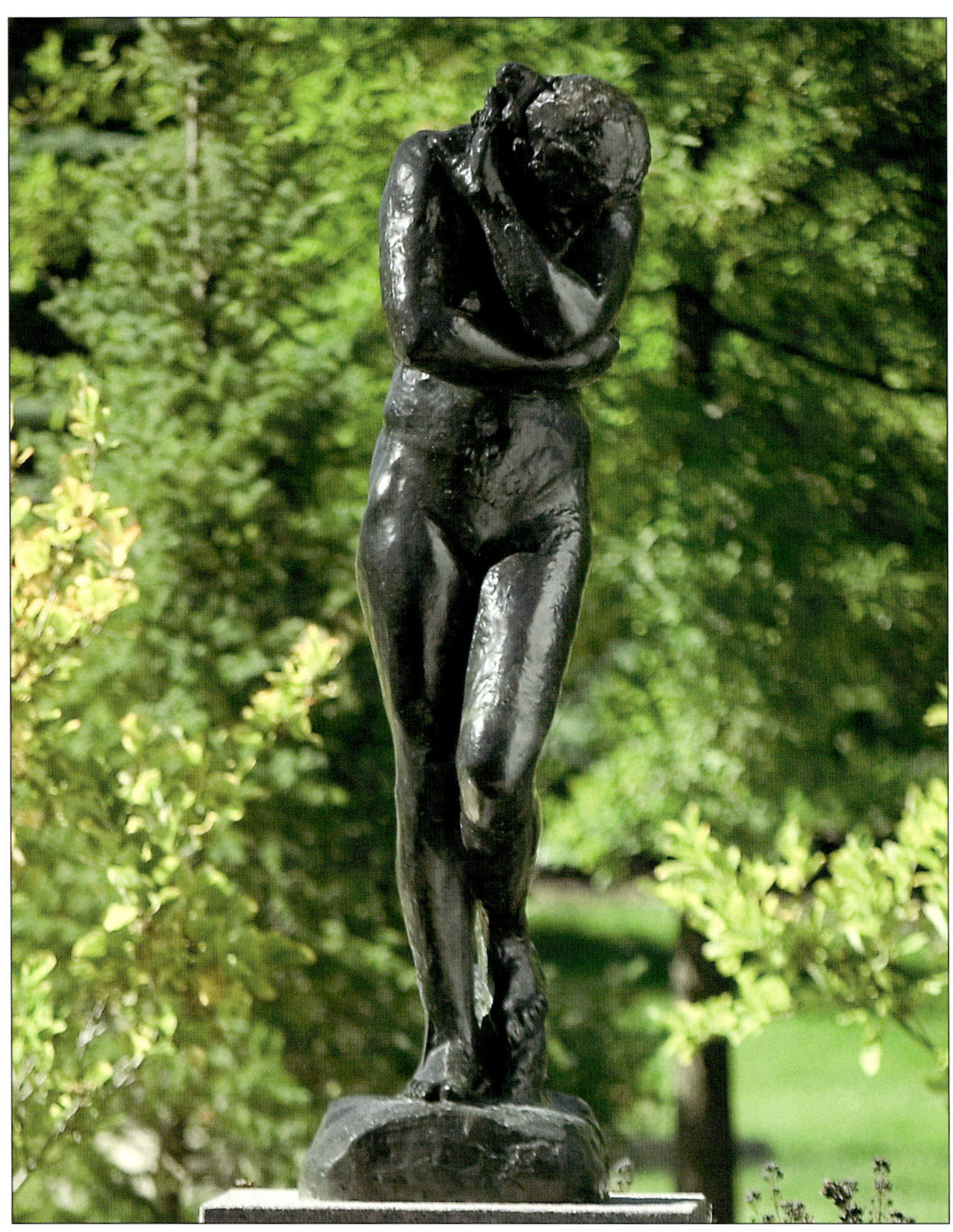

Auguste Rodin. *Eve*, 1881 (cast before 1920). Photo by William J. Hebert

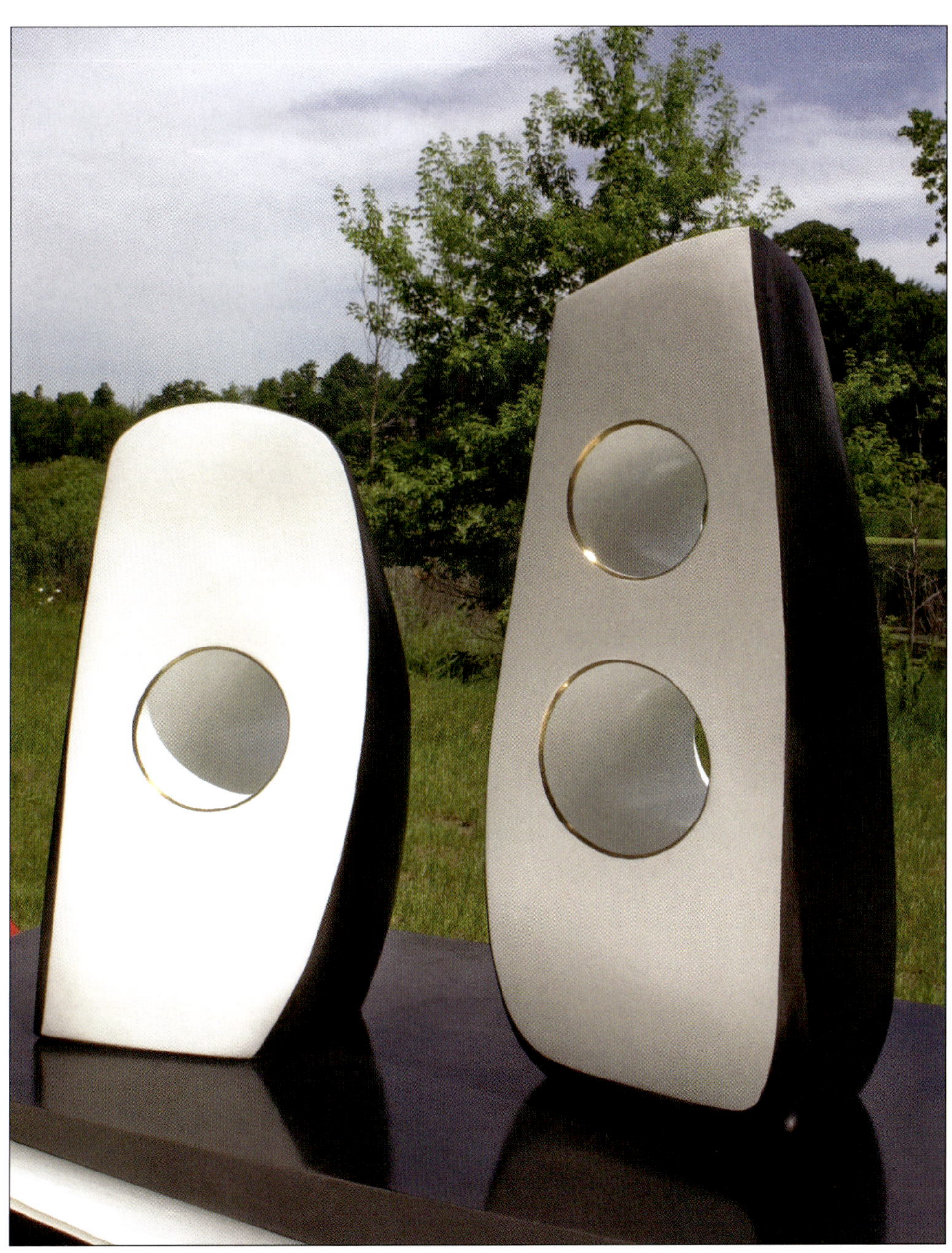

Barbara Hepworth. *Summer Dance*, 1971. © Alan Bowness, Barbara Hepworth Estate. Photo by Chuck Heiney

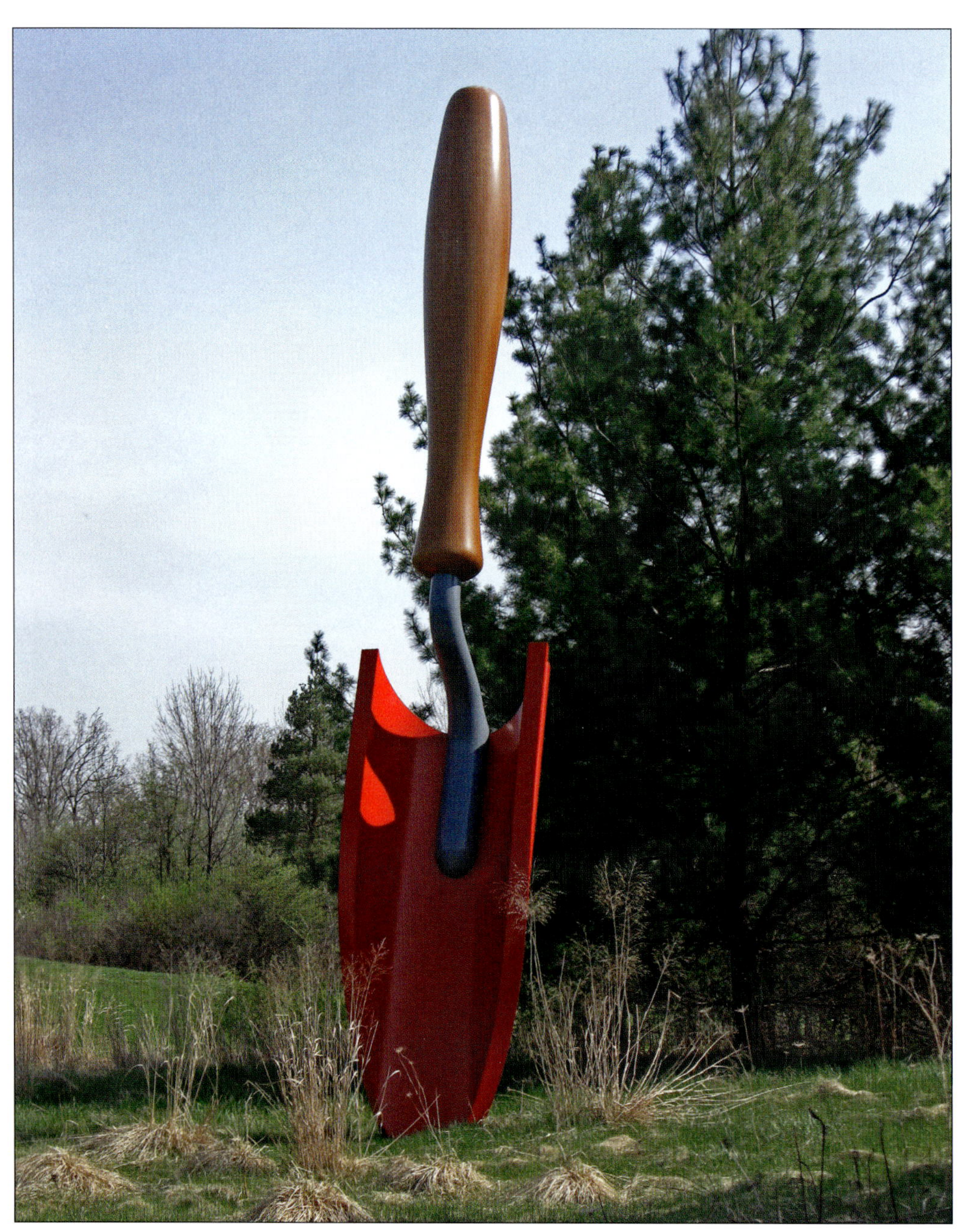

Claes Oldenburg and Coosje van Bruggen. *Plantoir,* 2001. Photo by Larry ten Harmsel

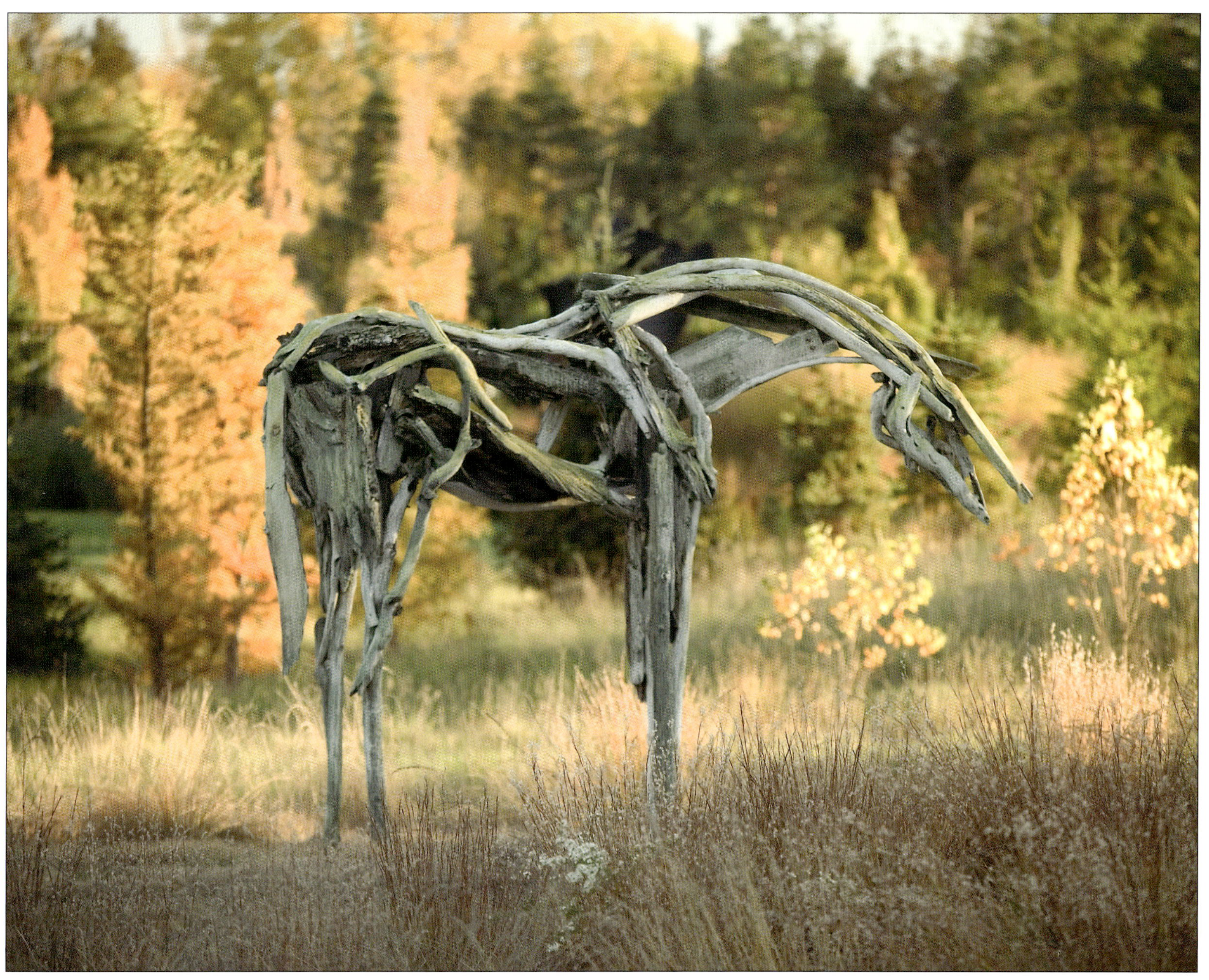

Deborah Butterfield. *Cabin Creek,* 1999. Photo by William J. Hebert

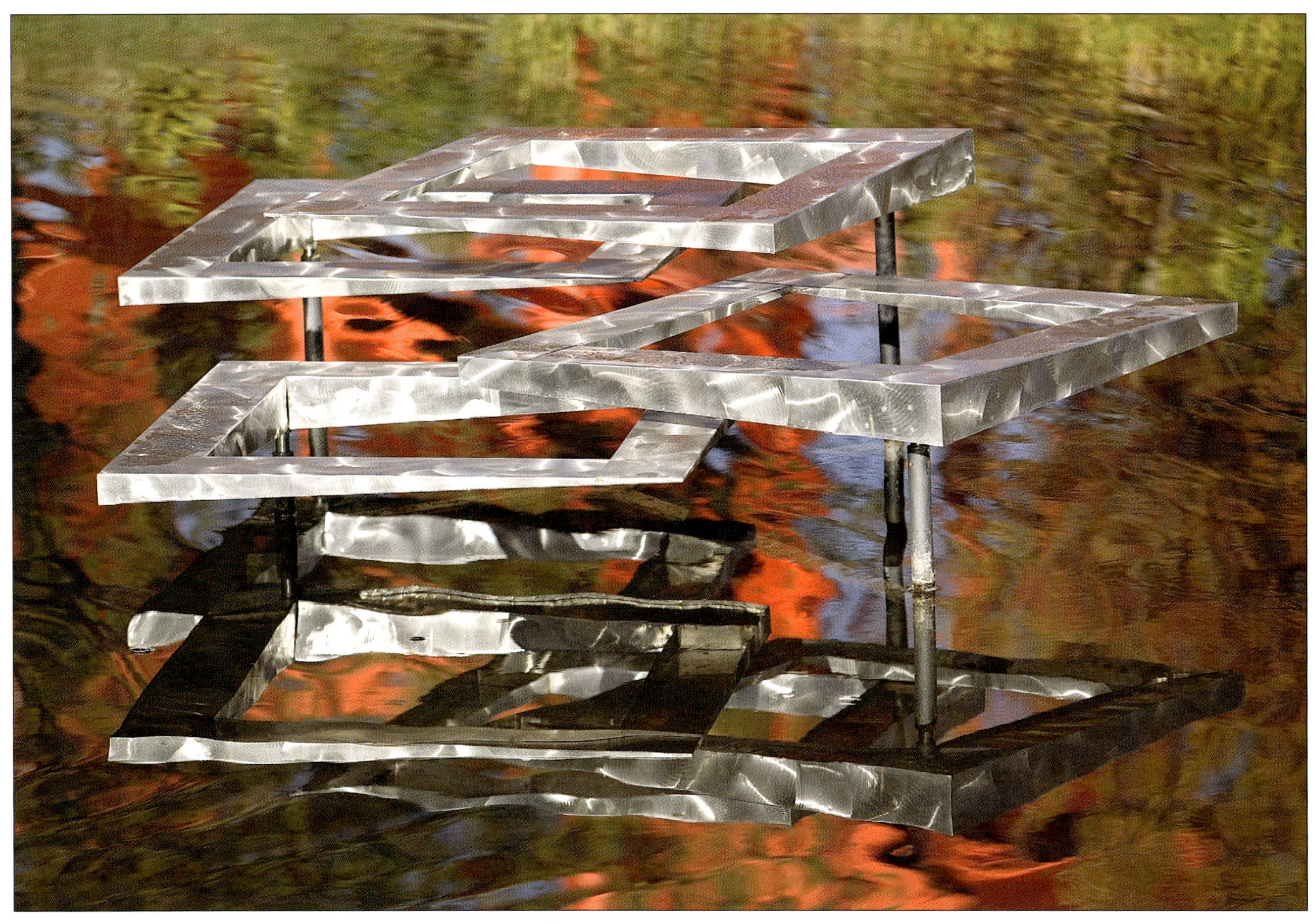

George Rickey. *Four Open Squares Horizontal Gyratory – Tapered,* 1984. Photo by William J. Hebert

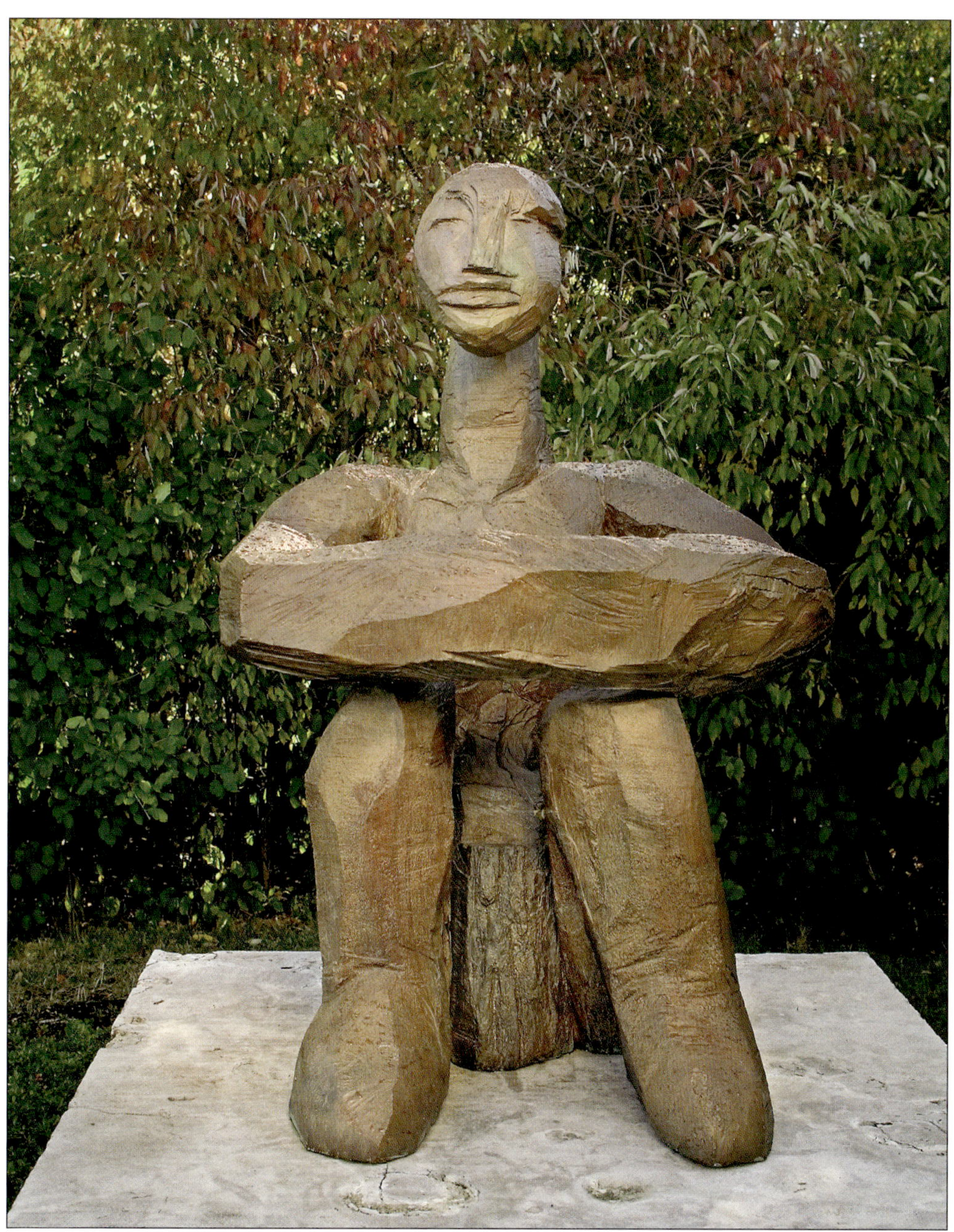

Dietrich Klinge. *Grosser TreFree*, 2000. Photo by Chuck Heiney

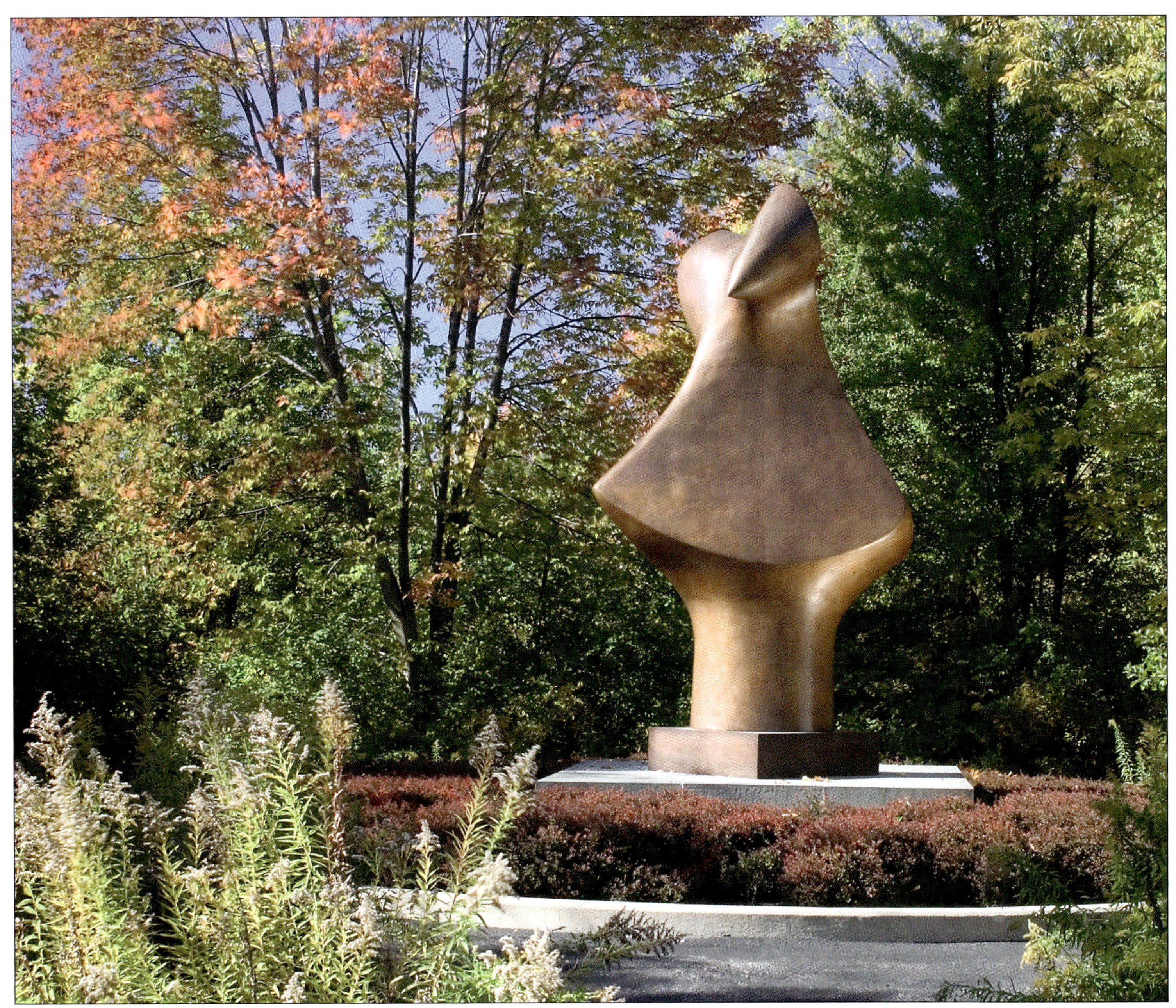

Henry Moore. *Bronze Form,* Cast 1985. Photo by William J. Hebert

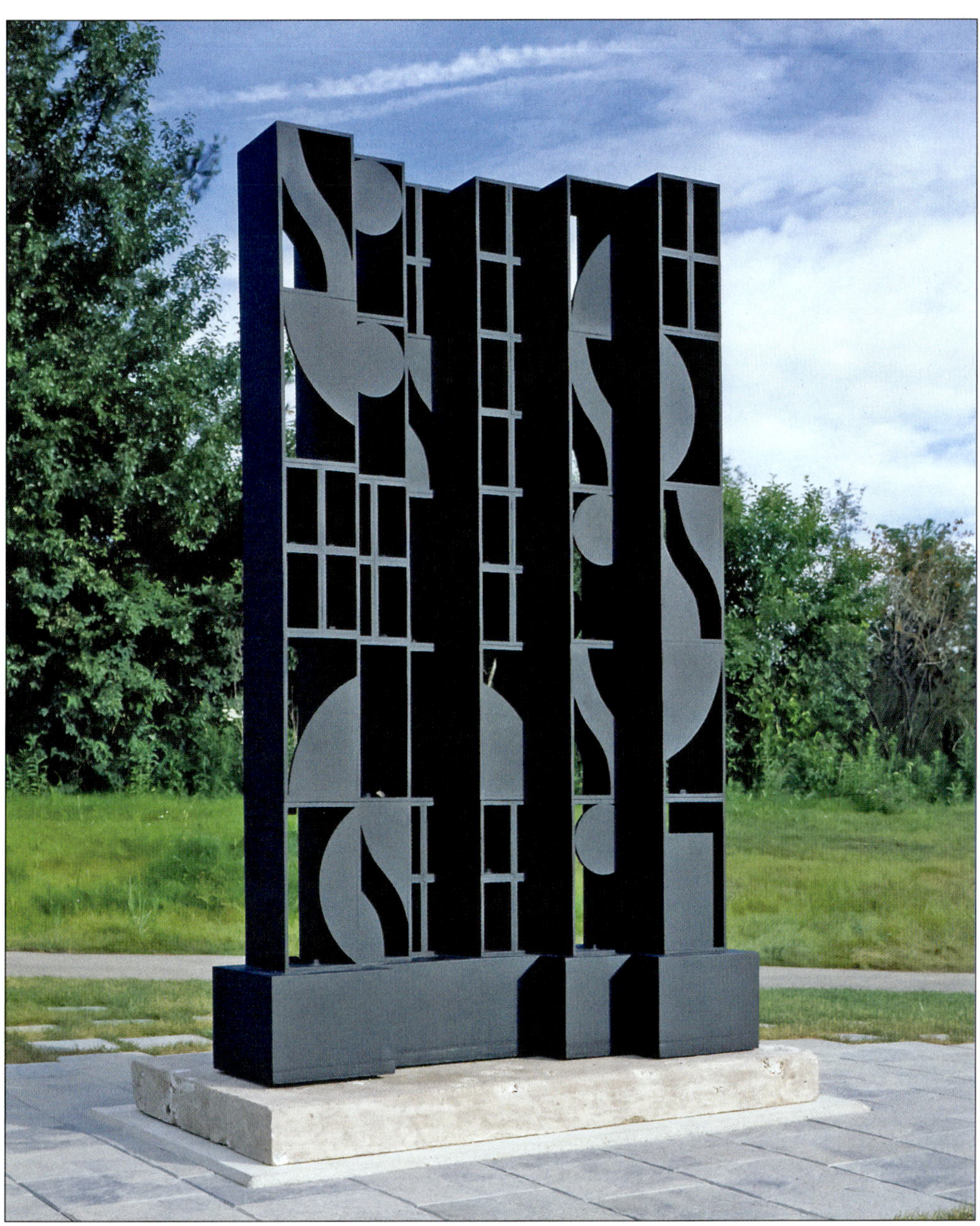

Louise Nevelson. ***Atmosphere and Environment XI*****, 1969.** © Estate of Louise Nevelson / Artists Rights Society (ARS), New York. Photo by William J. Hebert

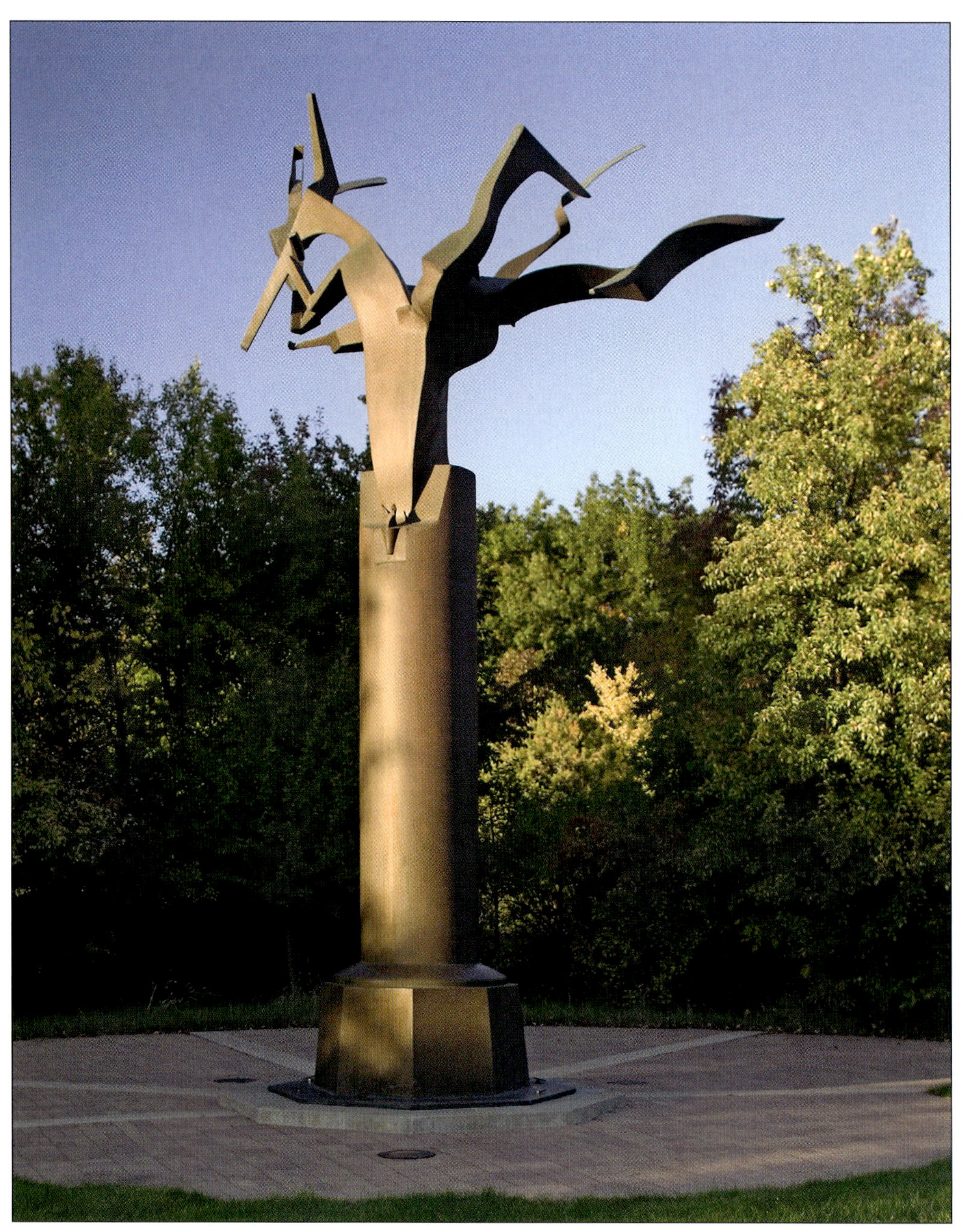

Richard Hunt. *Column of the Free Spirit,* 2000. Photo by William J. Hebert

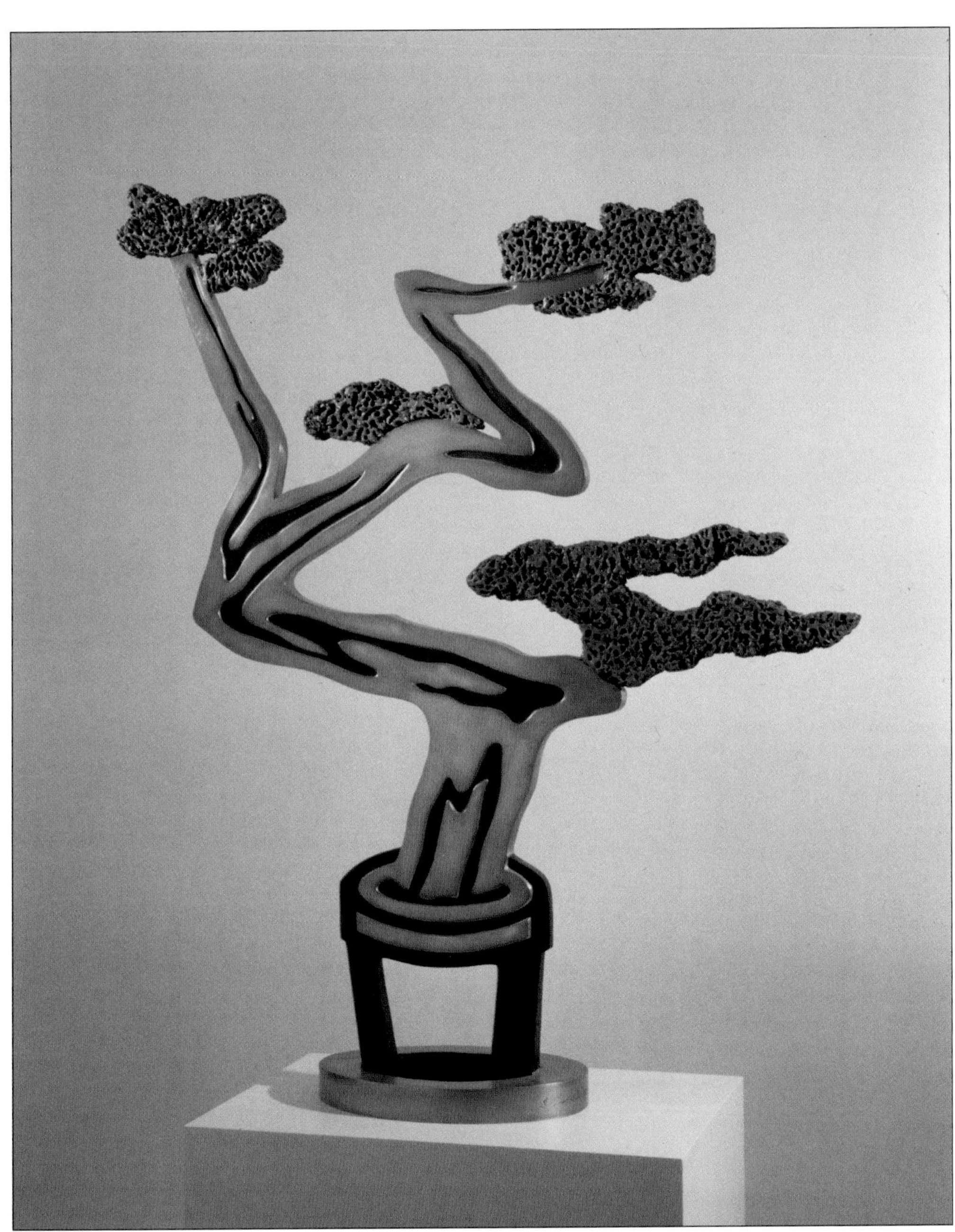

Roy Lichtenstein. *Bonsai Tree*, 1993. Photo by Chuck Heiney

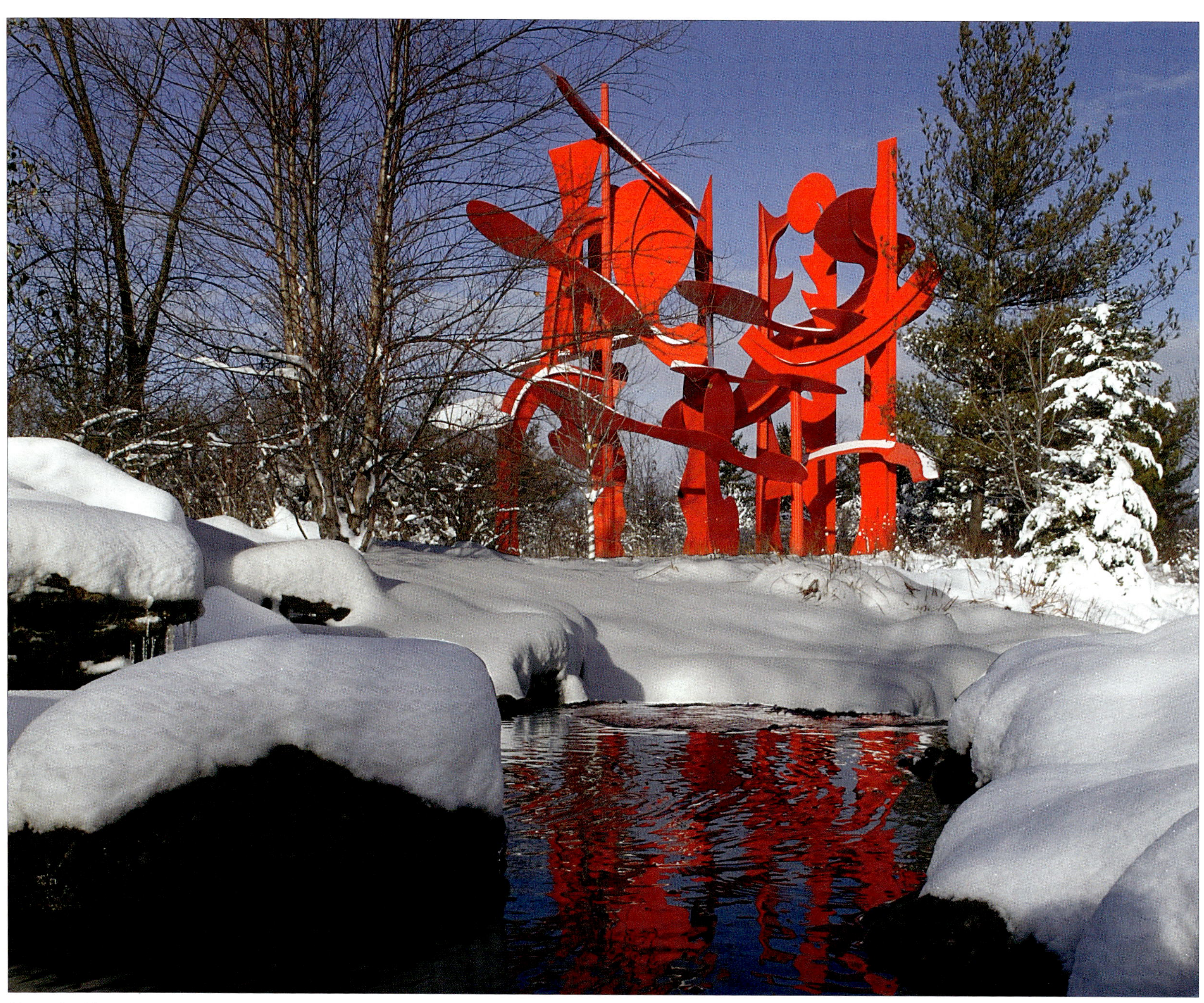

Alexander Liberman. *Aria*, 1979-1983. Photo by William J. Hebert